Ancient Messages

MW01613019

The god Ea in the watery *apsû*

Fig. 1. 7,000 years ago, in Babylonian mythology, there was a god named Ea (called Oannes by the Greeks). Ea was a water god and was depicted with the upper body of a man and the lower body of a fish. According to legends, Ea has been responsible for teaching everything that is human to Homo sapiens.

Ancient Messages

Timeless fragments of Ancient Wisdom, Great Knowledge & Mystical Experiences

NELL LANG

Lang Publishing Company
Texas • Florida

Author, Editor and Publisher: Nell Lang

ISBN 0-9722420-0-7

Copyright © 2004 by Nell Lang

All rights reserved. No part of this publication may be reproduced, or transmitted in any form, or by any means, electronic, or mechanical, including photocopy, recording, or any information storage and retrieval system, without permission in writing from the publisher.

Address for orders, editorial correspondence, and requests for permission to make copies of any part of the work should be mailed to:

Lang Publishing Company
908 Wren Ridge Drive
Grapevine, TX USA 76051
WWW Url: http://www.langpublishing.com
Email: nell@langpublishing.com
Telephone: 817-481-4931, Facsimile: 817-416-6876

Printed by Central Plains Book Manufacturing
Winfield, Kansas, United States of America

Front cover background photograph is a version of the painting *The Golden Bough* by the British artist Joseph Mallord William Turner (1775-1851), which title is taken from an incident in the *Aeneid*, courtesy of Tate Britain and *Encyclopedia Wikipedia*. **Back cover** photographs of Thoth and Oannes are courtesy of the *Canadian Museum of Civilization*. The Isis and Osiris photograph, courtesy of the website *Historical Records of Water-Beings* at http://www.water-consciousness.com.

Disclaimer. To the best of my knowledge, all quotations and pictures included herein fall under the fair use, or public domain guidelines of copyright law in the United States. All quotations and pictures remain the intellectual property of their respective originators. I do not assert any claim of copyright for individual quotations, or pictures. If you believe that any quotation, or picture violates a copyright you hold, or represent, we will immediately remove it upon notification pending good-faith resolution of any dispute. All quotations and pictures are the copyright of their respective owners and are provided here only for educational purposes.

I do assert a claim of copyright for my cover and layout design, compilation and selection of quotations, their unique scope and style, including order and placement of text and images.

This book and its contents are provided **as is.** I strive for accuracy but cannot be held responsible for any errors in quotations, incorrect attributions, or questionable spelling from times past. Some quotations may include content considered inappropriate by some standards for some age groups. I take no responsibility for filtering content based on any standards of morality, religion, or politics. Quoting someone does not necessarily mean that I approve of them, or their ideas, or agree with their words. By quoting authors I do not in any way mean to imply their endorsement, or approval of this book, or its contents.

Many of the quotations were verified using the Internet and the Internet addresses listed in the *Consulted Works* section were accurate at the time of publication. The inclusion of a Web site does not indicate an endorsement by the author, or Lang Publishing Company (LPC), and LPC does not guarantee the accuracy of the information presented at these sites.

Dedication

To a remarkable man, my husband, Michael L. Lang.
A man of renown integrity, intelligence, understanding and
compassion, and astonishing patience.

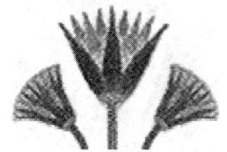

Acknowledgments

No one is luckier than I to have had the time and environment I needed to complete such an undertaking. To that I owe my sincere gratitude and appreciation to my husband, my best friend, patron, colleague, and mentor, Michael Lang. He has listened with phenomenal patience and an encouraging attitude to all the bits and pieces I have poured over him during the last few years of research and final preparation of the current style and selection presented in *Ancient Messages.* To him and my daughters, Skye and Kim, I would like to repay their love and encouragement.

I would like to thank and honor my mother, Ruby Lucille Cox Moreland (1919-1986), of proud Cherokee Indian ancestry, and my father, Raymond Moreland (1922-1987), a fourth generation Southern Baptist preacher, for the Lonesome Dove Baptist Church, in Grapevine, Texas. I thank them for encouraging me to be the best I could be and for giving me the love, courage and strength to make *somebody* of myself.

I would also like to thank Ellen Moreland, Darlene Gibbons, Matt and Dana DeVance, Jerry Campbell, Michelle and Jeff O'Brien, Bobby Rodgers, and Steve and Jeana Dupuis, for their help, support, encouragement, and for promoting and selling the first unprinted copies of *Ancient Messages*, without a clue as what the book was really about.

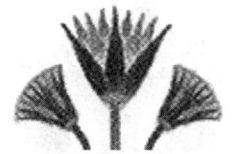

Introductory Note

"No part of a book is so intimate as the Preface. Here, after the long labor of work is over, the author descends from his platform, and speaks with his reader as man to man, disclosing his hopes and fears, seeking sympathy for his difficulties, offering defence or defiance, according to his temper, against the criticisms which he anticipates. It thus happens that a personality which has been veiled by a formal method throughout many chapters, is suddenly seen face to face in the Preface; and this alone, if there were no other reason, would justify a volume of Prefaces."

—P. F. COLLIER, HARVARD CLASSICS, PREFACES AND PROLOGUES TO FAMOUS BOOKS, VOL. 39.

Preface

Charles Nodier said, "Let us love ancient books, those immortal guardians of the epochs of great faith and of which there will soon be left behind no more than a legend."

I have been extremely fortunate to have been afforded the time to honor such worthy pursuits. In essence, this book was written to pay tribute to our civilization's most precious inheritance: our ancient heritage, and the authors of our ancient literature and historical accounts, without which we would not have the fabulous tales we take for granted today.

I eagerly accepted an opportunity to continue my work and to expand my knowledge of my beloved subjects, which include philosophy, ancient writing, languages and literature, ancient art, history and civilization, archaeology, geology, paleontology, cultural-anthropology, Egyptology, meteorology, to name a few, and was encouraged to complete the book I had discussed writing for a more than two decades. I decided to begin with an earlier version of *Ancient Messages*, entitled simply, *Arcana* (meaning hidden secret knowledge), and with a new title, a little different focus and look, *Ancient Messages began writing itself.*

This sacred and indispensable knowledge has leaped forward from the pages of ancient history, from their ancient monuments and breathtaking art and artifacts, praying to be released, read, spoken, written and rewritten, to be brought back to the lives of the living. I believe the spirit, or essence of these ancient authors has been speaking through me for years.

Ancient Messages is a glittering reservoir of tradition of all kinds, condensed anecdotes and hero-tales, curious quotations, and tales of mysterious times. The great knowledge that has been collected over the last several centuries, the historical records found in the histories of many Middle Eastern countries, the Bible, historical records and other religious documents are all we have of the ancient wisdom and great knowledge of the almost forgotten past.

Lord Bacon reminds us that:

"The earliest antiquity lies buried in silence and oblivion, excepting the remains we have of it in sacred writ. This silence was succeeded by poetical fables, and these, at length, by the writings we now enjoy; so that the concealed and secret learning of the ancients seems separated from the history and knowledge of the following ages by a veil, or partition-wall of fables, interposing between the things that are lost and those that remain. Many may imagine that I am here entering upon a work of fancy, or amusement, and design to use a poetical liberty, in explaining poetical fables…but this procedure has already been carried to excess; and great numbers, to procure the sanction of antiquity to their own notions and inventions, have miserably wrested and abused the fables of the ancients."

—LORD FRANCIS BACON, *ESSAYS*.

Collecting eighteenth and nineteenth century books has been more than a hobby for me for over thirty years. Some books in my collection have turned out to be quite rare in authorship, age and content, such as Thomas Gray's (1716-1771), *Elegy Written in a Country Churchyard and other poems* dated 1751, Oliver Goldsmith's (1728- 1771), *The Deserted Village*, published by Barse & Tompkins, New York in 1770, which is embellished with metallic gold leaf on the title page, printed one page at a time, on handmade paper, and undated.

Two important literary influences in my collection are *The History and Practice of Magic* by Paul Christian and Sir James George Frazer's *The Golden Bough,* which are bursting with legends, folklore, tales of mysticism, magic, and mysterious times. At the time I was reading these books, I worked for an Egyptian engineering firm and became increasing interested in ancient history, especially ancient Egypt and Mesopotamia. I found myself studying what is known as *The Royal Art.* The ancient *Hermetica*, the mystical wisdom that, together with the Kabbalah, formed the foundation of Western occultism. The term is derived from the surviving fragments of a multi-volume work known as the *Corpus Hermeticum*, or *Hermetica*.

This mystical philosophical work was allegedly written by Hermes Trismegistus (Thrice-Greatest) a mythical composite of the Egyptian god Thoth and the Greek god Hermes. The fragments present a synthesis of Kabbalistic, Neo-Platonic and Christian mystical and spiritual traditions and values.

According to legend, the Hermetic books were written on papyrus and stored in one of the great libraries in Alexandria. Most were lost when the ancient library burned. Surviving fragments supposedly were buried in a secret desert location known only to select initiates.

Ancient Messages revisits some of the sacred initiation rituals, ancient tradition, ancient wisdom, folklore, and myth and brings to light the *first and true ancient religion*, the one handed down to the Divine Plato from the Hermetic Philosophers of the Sacred Order of the Golden Dawn.

The secret knowledge and wisdom of our ancestors often pose a quandary for contemporary people. Moreover, modern philosophers who have been studying these ancient writings for years and still do not understand their true meaning. It was a time of secrecy, and their very survival depended on it. It seems that the ancients knew a lot about their world, far and wide, but sacred knowledge was available only to very few initiated *guardians* and *philosophers*. The guardians of The Rose Cross.

Hermes-Thoth (the Magi of Egypt) named it The Rose-Cross, Sphere of the Infinite:

"**I [Ioithi in the sacred language]** symbolizes the active creative principle and the manifestation of divine power that fertilizes matter.
N [Nain in the sacred language] symbolizes passive matter, the mold of all forms.
R [Rasith in the sacred language] symbolizes the union of these two principles and the perpetual transformation of created things.
I [Ioithi in the sacred language] symbolizes again the divine creative principle and signifies that the creative strength which emanates from it ceaselessly returns to it and springs from it everlastingly."

—ANTOINE COURT DE GEBELIN (1725-1784). HIS MAIN WORK, *THE PRIMITIVE WORLD ANALYZED, AND COMPARED TO THE MODERN WORLD*, WAS PUBLISHED 1772. *SEE* A. E. WAITE, *THE SECRET TRADITION IN FREEMASONRY.* —ED.

Dr. Stephen Colvin in 1914 wrote:

"What reply can we frame to the objection that myth is intellectually and morally wrong because it is not true? Our answer to this view of the case will be aided if we consider again the position which we have previously set forth, namely, that reality and truth depend on the agreement of our present experience with our total experience and the experience of others. *That which best fits into experience, which most uniformly satisfies the intelligence, is the truth; and since experience must never change, there is no truth that is absolute and that will stand the test of the ages.*"

—STEPHEN S. COLVIN, PH.D. *THE LEARNING PROCESS.* 1914:119.

In 1937, Nobel Prize winner Edmond Bordeaux Szekely wrote in his Foreword, "I have nothing to add to this text. It speaks for itself. The reader who studies the pages that follow with concentration, will feel the eternal vitality and powerful evidence of these profound truths which mankind needs today more urgently than ever before. 'And the truth shall bear witness of itself.'"

—EDMOND BORDEAUX SZEKELY, *THE ESSENE GOSPEL OF PEACE,* BOOK ONE, FOREWORD, LONDON, 1937.

It is not difficult to value the importance of these precious literary treasures and the brilliant men and women by which they were authored. I hope the reader enjoys *Ancient Messages* and finds at least one passage that fills them with wonder.

Nell Lang, July 26, 2004

Contents

1. Benjamin Disraeli (1804-1881)
2. Kamal Jumblatt (1917-1977)
3. Winston Churchill (1864 -1965)
4. Roger Bacon (1214 -1292)
5. Marsilius Ficino (15th century AD)
6. James the Just, *The First Apocalypse of James*
7. Publilius Syrus (c. 42 BC)
8. Francis Bacon (1561-1626), *Essays*
9. Publius Vergilius Maro (70-19 BC), *Celestial Virtues*
10. E. E. Rehmus, *Whales*
11. Nesta Webster, *Secret Societies*
12. *Die neresten Arbeiten des Spartacusund Philo in dem Illuminaten*
13. Artephius (200–1119), *The Secret Book*
14. Samuel L. Clemens, *Mark Twain's Notebook,* 1896
15. Gary K. North, *None Dare Call It Witchcraft*
16. *Psalm* 46
17. H. P. Blavatsky (1831-1891), *The Secret Doctrine*

18. Iamblichus (250-330), *On the [Egyptian] Mysteries*
19. Sir Arthur Charles Clark (1917-2001)
20. Bene Gesserit, *Axioms*
21. Ashok K. Gangadean, *Quest for the Primal Word*
22. Dr. Doreal, *The Emerald Tablets*
23. H. Schwartz, *How the Tenth Tribe Lost Its Words*
24. Ross Fuller, *On Listening and the Word*
25. Pope Saint Gregory, the Great (540-604)
26. Michael Angelo (1746-1801)
27. Benjamin Disraeli (1804-1881)
28. R. Schwaller DeLubicz (1887-1961), *Sacred Silence*
29. Plato (427-347 BC), *Republic*
30. Abraham Cohen, *Everyman's Talmud*
31. Plato (427-347 BC), *Timaeus*
32. Count Alessandro Cagliostro (1743-1795)
33. U. S. Andersen, *Three Magic Words*
34. Honoré de Balzac (1799-1850), *The Magic Skin*
35. Count Alessandro Cagliostro (1743-1795)
36. A. Saint-Yves d'Alveydre (1842-1909)
37. H. P. Blavatsky (1831-1891), *Isis Unveiled*
38. Elsa-Berita Titchenell, *The Mask of Odin*
39. Sir C. Leonard Woolley, *The Sumerians*
40. *Oannes and the Origins of Western Civilization*
41. Walter Baucum, *Tracing Dan*
42. H. P. Blavatsky (1831-1891), *The Secret Doctrine*
43. William Shakespeare (1564-1616)
44. *The Corpus Hermeticum* (c. AD 300)
45. Charles F. Berlitz, *The Bermuda Triangle*
46. Plotinus (204-270), The *Enneads*
47. *Libellus X. 24b-25, Corpus Hermetica*
48. Saint Augustine, *Civitas Dei*, XVIII. 29
49. S. Paul Burholt, *Sacred Threshold*
50. Gaius Julius Caesar (100-44 BC)
51. Tod Harris, *The Word Made Flesh*
52. H. P. Blavatsky (1831-1891), *The Races of Man*

53. Nikolaus Copernicus (1473-1543)
54. Francis Bacon (1561-1626)
55. F. Sherwood Taylor, historian of alchemy
56. Roger Bacon (1212-1292)
57. *Proverbs* 1-7
58. *Matthew* 13:34-35
59. *Luke* 8:9-10
60. E. E. Rehmus, *Wudjat Eye of Ra*
61. Ithell Colquhoun
62. Michael Maier, *Atalanta Fugiens,* 1618
63. H. P. Blavatsky (1831-1891), *The Secret Doctrine*
64. *Seasons of the Moon*
65. Grant R. Jeffrey, *The Signature of God*
66. E. E. Rehmus, *Slyphs*
67. Socrates and Glaucon, Plato's *Republic*

Chapter 2 – The Claiming of Atlantis   99

1. Kenneth L. Feder, *Frauds, Myths and Mysteries*
2. Helena P. Blavatsky (1831-1891), *The Races of Man*
3. Dr. Doreal, *Interpretation of the Book of Revelation*
4. Plato (427-347 BC), *Critias,* (360 BC)
5. Ignatius Donnelly, *Atlantis: The Antediluvian World*
6. A. Galanopoulos, *Atlantis: The truth behind the legend*
7. J. V. Luce, *Lost Atlantis: New light on an old legend*
8. Helena P. Blavatsky (1831-1891), *The Atlanteans*
9. Edgar Cayce, *Continent and Culture of Atlantis*
10. Helena P. Blavatsky, *The Races of Man*
11. Rainer W. Kühne, *The Location and Dating of Atlantis*

Chapter 3 – Tales of Creation, Emanation & Evolution

1. Ramon Gil Barros, *The Story of Noanase*
2. Helena P. Blavatsky (1831-1891), *Theosophy*
3. Swami Krishnananda, *Mandukya Upanishad, 1, 6*
4. *Koran* 27:15
5. René Guénon, *Language of the Birds*
6. Gil Ramon Barros, *Message to the Younger Brother*
7. Saint Bernard of Clairvaux (1090-1153)
8. *Mark* 11:24
9. King Solomon, *Ecclesiastes* 11
10. Akkadian version, *The Story of Atrahasis* (c. 1640 BC)
11. Assyrian version, *Epic Of Gilgamesh* (c. 650 BC)
12. *Matthew* 26:53
13. Hebrew version, *The Story of the Flood*
14. Robert Crosbie (1849-1919), *Theosophy Magazine*
15. Sumerian version, *The Epic of Gilgamesh*
16. Helena H. Blavatsky (1831-1891), *Theosophy*
17. E. F. Schumacher, *Enlightenment Magazine*
18. Chart of the Antediluvian Patriarchs and the Date of the Flood from Genesis
19. *Bereshith (Genesis) 1:1, The Torah*
20. E. E. Rehmus, *Sephiroth*
21. E. E. Rehmus, *Enochian*
22. Eliphas Levi, *The Nuctameron of the Hebrews*
23. Robert Temple, *The Sirius Mystery*
24. E. E. Rehmus, On *Angels*
25. Arthur Charles Clark, On *Creationism*, *In Science*
26. Mark Twain, *Mark Twain's Notebook*, 1896

1. Albert Einstein (1879- 1955)
2. Henry W. Longfellow (1807-1882), *The Builders*
3. Antoine Court de Gebelin (1725-1784)
4. Sir Isaac Newton (1643-1727)
5. Vincent Van Gogh (1853-1890)
6. Paul Valery (1871-1945), *Collected Works*
7. Charles Burchfield (1893–1967), American painter
8. Jerome Rothenberg, *Technicians of the Sacred: A Range of Poetries from Africa, America, Asia, Europe and Oceania,* Ancient Aztec song
9. Honoré de Balzac (1799-1850), *The Magic Skin*
10. James R. Lowell (1819-1891), *The Present Crisis*
11. Henry W. Beecher (1813-1887), *Progress of Thought in the Church*
12. Ralph Waldo Emerson (1803-1882), *Essays*
13. W. E. Channing, *Address on Self-Culture*
14. Stephen Vincent Benet, *The Making of a Dream*
15. Plato (427-347 BC), *Republic*
16. Khalil Gibran (1883-1931), *The Prophet*
17. Roger Bacon (1214-1292)
18. Francis Bacon (1573-1625), *Essay on Studies*
19. Madame Marie Curie (1867-1934)
20. Ludwig Von Beethoven (1770-1827)
21. Sir Thomas More (1478-1535), *Utopia,* 1515
22. Roger Ascham (1515-1568), *The Schoolmaster*, 1570
23. Francis Bacon (1573-1625), *Essay on Truth*
24. John Lyly (1554-1606), *Euphues: Anatomy of Wit*
25. John Milton (1608-1674), *Areopagitica,* 1644
26. Jaina Sutras, (trans) the *Prakrit* by Hermann Jacobi, 1884, from the *Sacred Books of the East*
27. Eminent scholar of Gnosticism, Elaine Pagels, *An Introduction To Gnosticism and The Nag Hammadi Library*

28. Ellen Boye, *Grönland*
29. Leonard Crow Dog, *American Myths and Legends*
30. John H. Wellington, *German Southwest Africa*, 1901
31. Rene Maunier, *The Sociology of the Colonies*
32. Max Ehrmann (1872-1945), *Desiderata*
33. David Appelbaum, *Can War Be Stopped?*
34. Fariduddin 'Attar (1130-1230)
35. S. Palacios i. Mendiburu, *Boletin de la Sociedad Geografica de Lima*, 1892
36. Michel de Nostradamus (1503-1566)
37. German Professor Boon
38. Plato (427-347 BC), *Phaedo,* (360 BC)
39. Ron Crocombe, *New Guinea*
40. *Bhagavad-Gita* xviii. 59
41. Persian saying
42. Miguel Chase-Sardi & Adolpho Colombres, *Por la Liberación del Indigena, Buenos Aires*
43. E. E. Rehmus, On *Easter Island*
44. Mel Watkins, *The Dene Declaration*
45. *Unidad Indigena*, 1975 1(1):1
46. Aristotle (384-322 BC)
47. Akhenaten (1370-1336 BC)
48. Thomas Paine

Chapter 5 – Tales of Ancient Egypt, Thoth-Hermes & Mercury

1. Aubrey De Sélincourt, *Arrian: Campaigns of Alexander*
2. William Kingsland, *Great Pyramid in Fact & Theory*
3. Manly Hall, *Freemasonry and the Ancient Egyptians*
4. William Henry, *The Language of the Birds*
5. Archimedes (287-212 BC)
6. *Grades of the Ancient, Primitive Rites of Freemasonry*

7. Iamblichus, *Treatise On the [Egyptian] Mysteries*
8. Sir E. A. Wallis Budge, *Egyptian Book of the Dead*
9. Count Alessandro Cagliostro (1743-1795)
10. Osiris Onnophris (c. 2400 BC), ancient king of Egypt
11. *Dream Stele of Tuthmosis*
12. Plato (427-347), *Republic*
13. Aleister Crowley, *Liber Aleph*
14. Aleister Crowley, *Liber Aleph* part 7
15. Sigmund Freud, *Moses and Monotheism*, 1938
16. Mike Fillon, *Science Solves the Ancient Mysteries*
17. *Osiris, Occultopedia*
18. E. E. Rehmus, On *Baghdad*
19. Manly Hall, *Freemasonry and the Ancient Egyptians*
20. William Kingsland, *The Great Pyramid in Fact*
21. Tod Harris, *The Word Made Flesh*
22. Sir E. A. Wallis Budge, *Egyptian Book of the Dead*
23. A. S. Mercatante, *Who's Who in Egyptian Mythology*
24. Dr. Doreal, *Preface to The Emerald Tablets*
25. Thoth, *Emerald Tablet No. 1, The History of Thoth*
26. Thoth, *Hundred Aphorisms of Thoth-Hermes*
27. Sir James George Frazer, *The Golden Bough*
28. Thoth, *Emerald Tablet No. 5, The Dwellers of Unal*
29. King Ashurbanipal of Assyria (668-627 BC)
30. Thoth, *Hundred Aphorisms of Thoth-Hermes*
31. Hermes Trismegistus, *Corpus Hermeticum*
32. A. S. Mercatante, *Who's Who in Egyptian Mythology*
33. Speech of Thoth, *The Pymander*
34. Thoth, *Keys to Life and Death*
35. Thoth, *Emerald Tablet No. 14, Supplemental*
36. *SHAZAM*
37. *The Goddess Isis*
38. *The Doctrine of Apollonius of Tyana*

Chapter 1

Tales of Ancient Wisdom, Great Knowledge & Mystical Experiences

Fig. 2. The Legend of Saint George and the Dragon. 'Every day,' said the old man, 'he demands the sacrifice of a beautiful maiden and now all the young girls have been killed. The King's daughter alone remains, and unless we can find a knight who can slay the dragon she will be sacrificed tomorrow. The king of Egypt will give his daughter in marriage to the champion who overcomes this terrible monster.'

"This book was written so

The wisdom of the wise, and the experience of ages,
may be preserved by quotation."[1]

—Benjamin Disraeli

"These texts are not addressed to common mortals,
Gnostic perception is a path reserved for the elite.
For in the Words of the Bible,

'Do not cast your pearls before swine.'"[2]

—Kamal Jumblatt

"It's a good thing that an uneducated man read a book of quotations."[3]

—Winston Churchill

"As for wealth,

the true man of science neither receives it nor seeks it....

If he frequented kings and princes he would easily find those

who would bestow on him honors and wealth.

But that would hinder him from pursing the great

experiments

in which he delights....

In his pursuit of knowledge the philosopher can remove even

the walls of his cell to the outermost limits of the world."[4]

—Roger Bacon, 11th century alchemist, philosopher

"He is called the first author of theology:
he was succeeded by Orpheus,
who came second amongst ancient theologians:
Aglaophemus,
who had been initiated into the sacred teaching of Orpheus,
was succeeded in theology by Pythagoras,
whose disciple was Philolaus,
the teacher of our Divine Plato.
Hence there is one *ancient theology*...
taking its origin in Mercurius
–Latin form of Hermes –
and culminating in the Divine Plato."[5]

–Marsilius Ficino, 15th century philosopher

"You have come with knowledge,
that you might rebuke their forgetfulness.
You have come with recollection,
that you might rebuke their ignorance."[6]

—James the Just says of Jesus
The First Apocalypse of James

28

"Speech is a mirror of the soul: as a man speaks, so is he."[7]

—Publilius Syrus, 1st century

"The divine philosopher declares:

God has made everything beautiful in its season;

and has given over the world to our disputes and inquiries;

but that man cannot find out the work which God has

wrought,

from its beginning up to its end."[8]

—Francis Bacon
The Essays; Counsels, Civil and Moral
of Francis Bacon

"Their natures fiery are, and from above,

And from gross bodies freed,

divinely move."[9]

−Publius Vergilus Maro, Roman poet
Vergil on the Celestial Virtues

"The Whale,

symbolizes the world; its huge,

unconscious better side or healthy nature.

A whale washed ashore dead

is an omen of uncontrollable disaster."[10]

—E. E. Rehmus
The Magician's Dictionary

"Our cause is a secret within a secret,
It is a secret only another secret can explain,
It is a secret that is veiled by a secret"[11]

—Nesta Webster
Secret Societies and Subversive Movements

"A cover is always necessary.
In concealment lies a great part of our strength.

Hence, we must always hide ourselves under the name of

another society."[12]

—Die nevesten Arbeiten des Spartacusund

Philo in dem Illuminaten

"...Are you so foolish as to believe we will openly teach you
the greatest and most important of secrets?
I assure you that anyone who attempts to study,
according to the ordinary and literal sense of their words,
what the Hermetic Philosophers write,
will soon find himself in the twists of a labyrinth
from which he will be unable to escape,
having no Ariadne's thread to lead him out."[13]

—Artephius, 12th century philosopher, teacher
The Secret Book

"The man who does not read good books has no advantage over the man who cannot read them."[14]

—Mark Twain

"Psychic goal is or basic urge is Gnostic.
Salvation through knowledge –
secret knowledge.

The power to direct and control personal development –
meaning that power is personal–
being to being."[15]

–Gary K. North
None Dare Call It Witchcraft

"God is our refuge and strength,

a very present help in trouble.

Therefore will not fear,

thought the earth be removed,

and though the mountains be carried into the midst of the

sea."[16]

— Psalm 46

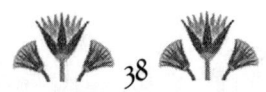

"Seven stands for dominion of soul over body or matter.

It is the number of knowledge,

often secret,

and of magic power.

Seven is associated with the ages of man,

the seven planets,

seven planes,

seven laws of nature,

and the seven days of the week.

Seven has always been a magic number."[17]

—Helena P. Blavatsky
The Secret Doctrine

"The angels or divine messengers,

servants of eternal Providence,

are spirits more perfect in essence than men.

They help us,

yet without restricting our will,

which is always free to choose between good and evil.

They work out the plan of the various ordeals to which

every human being is submitted during earthly life;

they give an account of our actions to God and lead our

souls after death into the region of rewards and expiations."[18]

—Jamblichus
Treatise, On the Egyptian Mysteries

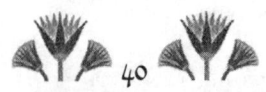

"Any sufficiently advanced technology is indistinguishable from magic."[19]

—Sir Arthur Charles Clarke

"Seek freedom and become captive of your desires.

Seek discipline and find your liberty."[20]

—Bene Gesserit
Axioms

"There is no contradiction in realizing that Logos[i]

is expressed in Yahweh,

Aum,

Tao, Sunyata,

Brahman,

Christ....

The dialogue of Logos can accommodate multiple

grammatical expressions.

Realization of this truth is of the utmost importance

for the evolution

and survival of humanity."[21]

—Ashok K. Gangadean
Quest for the Primal Word

---

[i] Meaning primal word.

"This particular verse has aroused more controversy than almost any other one verse in the Bible.

The number of the beast is the number of man,

not a man; the 'a' is an interpolation.

The number 666 is the vibratory number of the octave of

vibration along which man's thought travels.

The basic vibratory thought octave of all mankind is 666

million millions...

this is the universal thought octave of mankind."[22]

—Dr. Doreal

Interpretation of the Book of Revelation

"For years after the separation from their brothers,

the tenth lost tribe of Israel paused at dusk,

raised up their tents,

and could not agree on where to seek the promised land,

and one day when they assembled for prayer

no words sang out,

for somehow they had lost the word *open*,

and from that day on the scroll remained tightly closed.

Divining the fate this sign foretold,

the prophets so frightened the people that

no man dared lay with his wife.

Instead all stretched out alone and discovered the silence of

their empty hands,

and by morning they had lost the word *hold*.

Soon afterwards their wanderings were cut short.

Day after day they stayed in their tents and refused to

continue

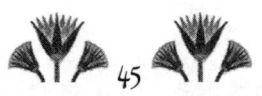

their journey.

At last they agreed that this place was their home,

and that day they lost the word search.

Before long not only the people,

but the animals,

the birds,

and even the winds had become silent.

And within a year

no one could speak the ancient tongue;

its words were scattered throughout the desert

like clouds of dust."[23]

—Howard Schwartz
Adams' Soul: The Collected Works of
Howard Schwartz

"The study of ancient texts brings contact with a different

mind

and feeling,

freeing us from a conditioning of which we are rarely

aware."[24]

—Ross Fuller
On Listening and the Word

"The discipline of silence is a kind of nourishment of the

Word...

by keeping silent We must learn to speak....

I hear What it is that I speak to you."[25]

–Pope Gregory the Great

"Do not trouble yourself too much with the light on your statue,

the light of the public square will test its value."[26]

—Michael Angelo to the young sculptor

"The secret of success is constancy of purpose."[27]

—Benjamin Disraeli

"Sacred or magical language is not to be understood as a succession of terms with definite meanings.

Actually,

the pronouncement of each sound of the language puts very precise nerves and breathings into action...

such physiological effects are evoked by the utterance of certain letters or words which make no sense in themselves.

The Pharaonic texts are rich in examples of litanies playing a magical role through the repetitions of sounds in words

and through word play...

although their transcription into our language is impossible since the pronouncement of this language is unknown."[28]

—R. A. Schwaller de Lubicz
Sacred Silence

"This, then,

which gives to the objects of knowledge their truth

and to him who knows them their power of knowing,

is the Form or essential nature of Goodness.

It is the cause of knowledge and truth;

and so while you may think of it as an object of knowledge,

you will do well to regard it as something beyond truth

and knowledge,

and precious these both are,

of still higher worth."[29]

—Plato
Republic VV 508

"Thirteen things are said concerning bread eaten in the

morning:

it protects from heat,

cold,

injurious spirits,

and demons;

it makes the simple wise and help him to win a lawsuit,

assists him to learn and teach Torah,

causes his utterances to be listened to,

his study remains with him,

his flesh does not exhale a bad odour,

he is attached to his wife and does not lust after another

woman;

it destroys tapeworms,

and some add,

it drives forth envy and causes love to enter."[30]

—Abraham Cohen, Everyman's Talmud

How mankind lost the ancient knowledge.

"There upon one of the priests,

who was of a very great age, said:

O Solon, Solon,

you Hellenes are never anything but children,

and there is not an old man among you,

in mind you are all young;

there is no old opinion handed down among you by ancient

tradition,

nor any science which is hoary with age.

And I will tell you why.

There have been,

and will be again,

many destructions of mankind arising out of many causes;

the greatest have been brought about by the agencies of fire

and water,

and other lesser ones by innumerable other causes,

and leaves only those of you who are destitute

of letters and education;

and so you have to begin all over again like children,

and know nothing of what happened in ancient times,

either among us or among yourselves."[31]

—Plato, Timaeus

"Do not smile, gentlemen.

My conviction in this respect cannot falter,

for it is based on fairly numerous experiments and on proofs

too striking to be ignored.

Yes, each one of us is named in the heavens

at the same time as on earth,

this, predestinated, bound,

by the occult laws of increate Wisdom,

to a series of more or less fatal ordeals before he has even

made the first step towards his unknown future."[32]

—Count Alessandro Cagliostro

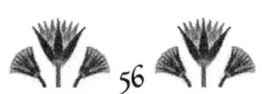

"*Basic thing behind all form,*

all creation,

is energy,

searching to attain movement in an intelligent existence

or intelligent direction."[33]

—U. S. Andersen
Three Magic Words

"As to whether a soul develops a connection between

fortunes

and wishes of possession,

Wishes fulfilled at the expense of your own life.

The more lavish the wishes weighs on the number of days of

your life from least to highest."[34]

―Honoré De Balzac
The Magic Skin

"The seven spirits of the Rose Cross,
guardians of the sacred key to the past and future will lay on
your forehead
the crown of the Master of Time.
Initiation for the Crown of Knowledge
was based on twenty-two tests.
The twenty-two Arcana were tests of total,
unequivocal faith in the Divine Being.
Tests were held inside the Sphinx.
The opening was brass with secret spring
only known to the Magi."[35]

—Count Alessandro Cagliostro

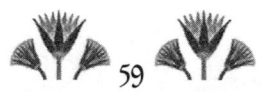

"In certain regions of the Himalayas,

among the twenty-two temples that represent the twenty-two

Arcana of Hermes

and the twenty-two letters of some sacred alphabets,

Agarttha forms the mystic Zero,

which cannot be found....

A colossal chessboard that extends beneath the earth,

through almost all the regions of the Globe."[36]

—Saint-Yves d'Alveydre
Mission de l'Inde en Europe

"In those days,

in addressing their gods in their own language this language is

that of incantations or Mantras,

as they are called in India,

sound being the most potent and effectual magic agent,

and the first of the keys which opens the door of

communication between

Mortals and the Immortals."[37]

–Helena P. Blavatsky
Isis Unveiled

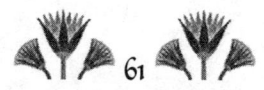

"Hear me, all ye holy kindred,
Greater and lesser sons of Heimdal!
You wish me to tell the ancient tales,
O Father of seers,
the oldest I know.

I remember giants born in the foretime,
They who long ago nurtured me;
Nine worlds I remember, nine trees of life,
Before this world tree grew from the ground."[38]

—Elsa-Brita Titchenell
The Masks of Odin

"Sumerian writing is the oldest,
sophisticated form of writing in existence,
having first appeared in about 3400 BC,
but it is neither crude nor primitive,
and there is no region on Earth which identifies any scribal
concept that might have been its forerunner.
It appeared in a complete and composite form,
as if from another world,
in the style known as cuneiform, wedge-shaped.
This was a series of angular phonetic symbols,
cuneates, ostensibly abbreviated from the pictographs
of the Sumerian temple priests."[39]

—Sir C. Leonard Woolley
The Sumerians

"Oannes,

according to Sumerian history,

introduced written language in the

Mesopotamian Valley over 5,000 years ago.

Many assume Oannes was merely a myth or legend of

the Sumerians,

others believe that he visited Earth from an extraterrestrial

source,

even others believe that he originated in a place like

the mythical Atlantis.

Oannes best be considered as a traveler from a pre-existing

civilization somewhere on Earth.

According to legend,

At Babylon there was a great resort of people of various

nations who inhabited Chaldaea and lived in a lawless

manner like the beasts of the field.

In the first year there appeared from that part of the

Erythraean sea which borders Babylonia,

64

an animal destitute of reason,

by the name of Oannes,

whose whole body was that of a fish.

That under the fish's head he had another head,

with feet also below,

similar to those of a man,

subjoined to the fish's tail.

His voice too, and language was articulate and human.

And a representation of him is preserved even to this day.

This Being was accustomed to pass the day among men;

but took no food at that season;

and he gave them an insight into letters and sciences,

and arts of every kind.

He taught them to construct cities,

to found temples, to compile laws,

and explained to them the principles of geometrical

knowledge.

He made them distinguish the seeds of the earth,

and showed them how to collect the fruits;

in short,

he instructed them in everything which could tend to soften

manners and humanize their lives.

From that time,

nothing material has been added by way of improvement to his

instructions.

And when the sun had set,

this Being Oannes,

retired again into the sea, and passed the night in the deep;

for he was amphibious.

After this there appeared other animals like Oannes." [40]

—Berossus, Babylonian priest 3rd century BC

Similarities of the
Hopi Indian and Hebrew Language

"Hopi u and Hopitu

meaning peaceful ones;

note similarity to

Habiru and Hebrew,

i.e., moqui.

Ojibwa Anishinabe

means first people.

Note: *ish* is Semitic for human being."[41]

—Walter Baucum
Tracing Dan

"The method which leads to absolute Truth is the one used and taught by the Great Teachers of Theosophy in all ages.

It may be stated in three words:

Man, Know Thyself.

It is the method of Spirit,

proceeding on the axiom that the whole manifested Kosmos,

visible and invisible,

is embodied consciousness, which can be known only through

the state of consciousness within man himself.

The process of knowing is one of ever greater self-realization,

or a series of progressive awakenings,

culminating in complete self-realization."[42]

—Helena P. Blavatsky
The Secret Doctrine

"Your thoughts, those that predominate,

determine your character, your career,

indeed your everyday life.

Thus it becomes easy to understand what is meant by the

statement that a man's thoughts make or break him.

And when we realize that there can be no action or reaction,

either good or bad,

without the generating force of thought initiating it,

the Biblical saying,

'For whatsoever a man soweth, that shall he also reap,

'There is nothing either good or bad,

but thinking so,

become more intelligible.'"[43]

—William Shakespeare

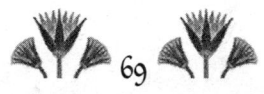

"Once on a time,

when I had begun to think about the things that are,

and my thoughts had soared high aloft,

while my bodily senses had been put under restraint by sleep –

yet not such sleep as that of men weighed down by fullness of

food or by bodily weariness –

methought there came to me a Being of vast and boundless

magnitude,

who called me by my name, and said to me,

'What do you wish to see and hear,

and to learn and come to know by thought?'

'Who are you?' I said.

'I,' said he, 'am Poimandres, the sovereign mind

⌒nous⌒.'

'I wish to learn,' said I, 'the things that are,

and understand their nature,

and get knowledge ⌒gnonai⌒ of God.'

'These,' I said, 'are the things of which I wish to hear.'

70

He answered, 'I know what you wish for,
for indeed I am with you everywhere;
keep in mind all that you desire to learn,
and I will teach you.'"[44]

—This is how the reader first enters the
Corpus Hermeticum

"The Piri Re'is Map found in Istanbul in 1929,
part of a world map said to have been copied from a Greek
original in the Library of Alexandria.
Among other features,
the Piri Re'is map shows detailed features of
Antarctica evidently drawn several thousand years
before Antarctica was discovered,
as well as the true shape of Antarctica without the covering
ice.
Other features indicate an advanced knowledge of
astronomy, trigonometry,
and the ability to determine longitude,
not known to our culture until the reign of George III of
England."[45]

—Charles F. Berlitz
The Bermuda Triangle

"Knowledge of the One is achieved through the

experience of its power and its nature,

which is to provide a foundation and location for all existents.

The power of the One is not a power in the sense of

physical, or even mental action;

the power of One,

is to be understood as the only adequate description of the

manifestation of a supreme principle that,

by its very nature,

transcends all predication and discursive understanding."[46]

—Plotinus, 2nd century AD

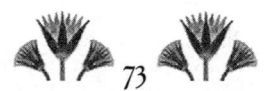

"For man is a being of divine nature;

he is comparable,

not to the other living creatures on earth,

but to the gods in heaven,

or at any rate he equals them in power.

None of the gods in the heaven will ever quit heaven,

and pass its boundary, and come down to earth;

but man ascends even to heaven and measures it;

and what is more than all besides,

he mounts to heaven without quitting the earth;

to so vast a distance can he put forth his power.

We must not shrink then from saying that

a man on earth is a mortal god,

and that a god in heaven is an immortal man."[47]

—Lebellus X. 24b-25
Corpus Hermetica

74

"As for morality,
it stirred not in Egypt until Trismegistus's time,
who was indeed long before the sages and philosophers of
Greece,
but after Abraham,
Isaac,
Joseph,
yea and Moses also;
for at the time when Moses was born, was Atlas,
brother of Prometheus,
a great astronomer, living,
and he was grandfather by the mother's side to the elder
Mercury,
who begat the father of this Trismegistus."[48]

—Saint Augustine, Civitas Dei, XVIII. 29

"For the ancients...

measurements of time were not abstract

but part of the warp and woof of human experience,

such as the setting sun,

the phases of the moon,

the tides,

the crowing of the cock,

the pattern of the seasons."[49]

–S. Paul Burholt
Sacred Threshold

*"Remember citizens,
that I am descended from Ancus Martius,
one of your ancient kings,
and that my ancestress Julia was the daughter of Venus."*[50]

—Gaius Julius Caesar

"The twenty-two letters of the Hebrew alphabet make
up a symbolic system that,
if manipulated correctly,
reveal not only the secret laws of the universe,
but of God himself."[51]

–Tod Harris
The Word Made Flesh

"Time is only an illusion produced by the succession of our states of consciousness as we travel through eternal duration....
According to the ancient doctrines, every member of this varied ethereal population, from the highest – Gods – down to the soulless Elementals, was evolved by the ceaseless motion inherent in the astral light.
Light is force, and the latter is produced by the Will.
As this Will proceeds from an intelligence which cannot err, for it is absolute and immutable and has nothing of the material organs of human thought in it,
being the superfine pure emanation of the One Life itself, it proceeds from the beginning of time, according to immutable laws, to evolve the elementary fabric requisite for subsequent generations of what we term human races."[52]

–Helena P. Blavatsky
The Races of Man

79

"The Sun...

In the middle of all sits the Sun, enthroned.

In this most beautiful temple,

could we place this luminary in any better position from which

he can illuminate the whole at once?

He is rightly called the Lamp, the Mind,

the Ruler of the Universe.

Hermes Trismegistus names him the Visible God,

Sophocles Electra calls him the All-seeing.

So the Sun sits as on a royal throne ruling his children,

the planets which circle round him."[53]

—Nikolaus Copernicus

"The virtue of prosperity is temperance,

of adversity fortitude,

Which in morals is the more heroical virtue.

Prosperity is the blessing of the Old Testament,

adversity the blessing of the New,

Which carrieth the greater benediction and the clearer

revelation

of God's favor."[54]

—Francis Bacon

Essays; Counsels, Civil and Moral of Francis

Bacon

"The hopeless pursuit of the practical transmutation of
metals was responsible for almost the whole of the
development of chemical technique
before the seventeenth century,
and further led to the discovery of many important materials.
This is the commonly recognized contribution of alchemy."[55]

—F. Sherwood Taylor
Distinguished historian of alchemy

"And God wishes all men to be saved and no man to perish,

and His goodness is infinite;

He always leaves some way possible for man through which he may be urged to seek his own salvation....

For this reason the goodness of God ordained that revelation would be given to the world that the human race might be saved....

And it is not surprising that the wisdom of philosophy is of this kind since this wisdom is only a general revelation made to all mankind because all wisdom is from God."[56]

—Roger Bacon

"*Let the wise listen and add to their learning,*

and let the discerning get guidance,

for understanding proverbs and parables,

the sayings and riddles of the wise."[57]

—Proverbs 1:6-7

What were the reasons for hiding this highest wisdom from the commoners?

"It is not easy to penetrate the inner meaning of the Bible,
which is the heavily veiled word of God.
Jesus spoke all these things to the crowd in parables;
he did not say anything to them without using a parable.
So was fulfilled what was spoken through the prophet:
I will open my mouth in parables,
I will utter things hidden since the creation of the world."[58]

—Matthew 13:34-35

"His disciples asked him what this parable meant.

He said,

The knowledge of the secrets of the kingdom of God has

been given to you,

but to others I speak in parables, so that,

though seeing, they may not see;

though hearing,

they may not understand."[59]

—Luke 8:9-10

" *Wudjat,*

The eye is the eye of Ra,

which in hieroglyphics means to make or create.

The symbol on the U.S. dollar bill was suggested by

the founders of America,

who were not Christians,

but Freemasons and occultists.

Superficially it means that whatever we do must be inspired

by superconscious insight,

not by petty quests for private power or selfish profit." [60]

—*E. E. Rehmus*
The Magician's Dictionary

"Yeats and the Celts before him, fidchell,
had a chessboard representing the four gates to the cities of
the four elements and in which the squares were cromlechs
– mystic, upright stones.

Gwenddolen,
in Arthurian legend,
is said to have possessed an enchanted chessboard that played
by itself."[61]

—Ithell Colquhoun

"He who attempts to penetrate into the Rose Garden of the Philosophers without the key resembles a man who would walk without feet."[62]

— Michael Maier
Atalanta Fugiens, 1618

"Great White Lodge,

a hierarchy of adepts who form the inner government of the

world,

guided by Secret Chiefs.

Mather's and Crowley's Golden Dawn was

supposedly the first outer brotherhood and its Temple

Masters were considered members.

The Rosicrucians were the second order

and the Silver Star

A∴A∴ the third and innermost order."[63]

–Helena P. Blavatsky
The Secret Doctrine

"Gate 49 - When the Jewish People left Egypt,

they were hovering over the precipice of spiritual annihilation.

They were at the last gate.

49 gates of tuma ⌒spiritual impurity⌒ exist in this world

and the Jewish People were at the threshold of oblivion.

49 is 7 times 7.

When you square a number, it reaches its ultimate

expression. It is the thing times itself;

nothing can be a greater revelation of essence than that.

Thus, 49 is the furthest reach of seven-ness in this world.

And seven is this world:

There are seven notes in the scale,

seven days in the week and seven colors in the rainbow.

Seven in Sound.

Seven in Time.

Seven in Space." [64]

—Seasons of the Moon

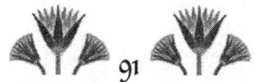

91

"Just as the number seven is found repeatedly hidden
beneath the text of Scripture,
we find the same number used repeatedly by the Creator in
His physical creation of the universe and its inhabitants.
There are precisely seven colors in the light spectrum that
merge together to form light.
The study of music again reveals that there are exactly
seven musically whole tones in the scale.
Every eighth musical note creates a new higher octave
repeating the pattern of seven tones.
The seven colors correspond to the seven musical notes.
In another manifestation of design,
the whole human body is effectively renewed at the cellular
level every seven years.
By the end of seven years almost every single cell of our
flesh, organs and bones will be replaced with new cells
manufactured according to an incredibly complex genetic
program in our DNA.

Our blood pulse rate slows down noticeably every seven

days throughout our life.

The gestation cycle to produce a baby takes 280 days

7 x 40.

Our lives are marked with the number seven

as God commanded us to rest every seventh day and noted

that our life expectancy is seventy years 7 x 10.

Almost all of the animals have gestation periods that are

multiples of seven:

lion, 98 days; sheep, 147 days; hens, 21 days; ducks, 28 days;

cats, 56 days; dogs, 63 days.

The number seven in Hebrew is derived from the root

word meaning:

to be full, satisfied, or have enough of,

while another meaning of the root is to swear,

or to make an oath.

We find seven appearing on the surface of the biblical text

as well as in prominent places,

93

including the seven spirits or manifestations of God:

the seven-fold blessing of Abraham, Gen 12:2,3;

God's seven-fold covenant with Israel, Exo 6:6-8;

and the marvelous design of sevens found in the

Book of Revelation.

John describes seven groups of seven in his Apocalypse

including:

7 churches, 7 seals, 7 trumpets, 7 vials, 7 personages, 7 dooms

and 7 new things." [65]

—Grant R. Jeffrey
The Signature of God

"Sylphs, the air elementals,

capable of changing their sizes and shapes fantastically,

who have the power of moving easily from dimension to

dimension.

They are lovely,

ethereal entities whose purpose is to inspire and instruct us.

We attract them by being clever and quick-witted and repel

them by being shallow or capricious.

They must always be allowed their freedom.

The nature of sylphs is such that although they can easily

be caught and pinned down –

indeed they appear eager to be bound by us mortals –

once so captured their beauty instantly fades and they very

quickly die.

They are as fragile as snowflakes and the other elements

quickly annihilate or absorb them.

The word has been traced to Greek *silphe*,

used by Aristotle to mean a kind of dubious beetle,

but its origin is likely to be Arabic *salafa*,

to boil away, or *salifat*, a natural trait.

The ballet, *La Sylphide* demonstrates all of this

perfectly,

Les Sylphides is merely a choreography without a

story.

The Donning encyclopedia describes sylphs as being

highly developed, feminine Intelligences.

A sylph may associate herself with an individual at birth

and help her, him to grow in non-materialistic ways,

to develop his individual freedom and to provide energy in

emergencies.

Perhaps the best way to think of a sylph is as a person's

genius."[66]

—E. E. Rehmus
The Magician's Dictionary

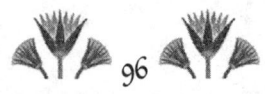

"Those then who know not wisdom and virtue,

and are always busy with gluttony and sensuality,

go down and up again as far as the mean;

and in this region they move at random throughout life,

but they never pass into the true upper world;

thither they neither look,

nor do they ever find their way,

neither are they truly filled with true being,

nor do they taste of pure and abiding pleasure.

Like cattle,

with their eyes always looking down and their heads stooping

to the earth, that is,

to the dining-table,

they fatten and feed and breed, and,

in their excessive love of these delights,

they kick and butt at one another with horns and hoofs which

are made of iron;

and they kill one another by reason of their insatiable lust.

97

For they fill themselves with that which is not substantial, and the part of themselves which they fill is also unsubstantial and incontinent."[67]

—Socrates to Glaucon
Plato's Republic

Chapter 2

The Claiming
of Atlantis

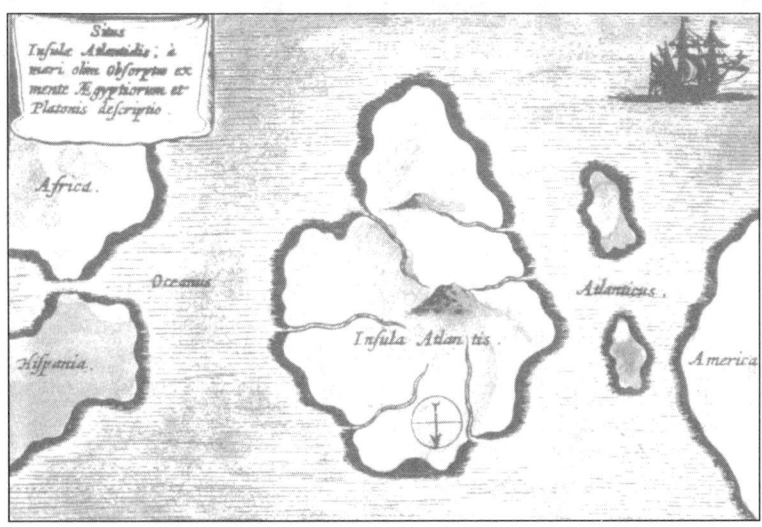

Fig. 3. Ancient Egyptian Map of Atlantis reproduced by Athanasius Kircher (1601-1680), a Jesuit priest, in his book *Mundus Subterraneus* in 1655. This is a view drawn looking downward from the north and facing south. The Latin inscription on the top left hand corner of the map of Atlantis translates: "Site of Atlantis now beneath the sea according to the believes of the Egyptians and the description of Plato."

Of all the world's unsolved puzzles, Atlantis is probably the biggest, exerting a mysterious influence over humankind for thousands of years. The passage of time has not diminished interest in the fabled continent, nor have centuries of skepticism by scientists and scholars succeeded in banishing it to obscurity.

"In the beginning,

Atlantis was an exquisite land of peaceful,

fair-haired, artistic, and intelligent people.

A perfect society, a divine society,

which shaped the most magnificent civilization

humankind has ever known.

The cities of Atlantis were said to be splendid places,

interconnected with blue canals and bordered by towers of

precious stones and orichalcum gently reaching skyward.

The astonishing achievements of the prehistoric world can be

traced to the brilliance of this curious ancient land.

The cultures of the ancient Egyptians and the Maya,

the civilizations of China and India,

the Inca, the Moundbuilders, and the Sumerians

were all derived from this source of civilization....

After a very long time on earth,

the 'divine portion' of their ancestry became diluted and the

human portion became domineering.

The result was a decadent society of depraved and

greedy people.

The dialogue relates that Zeus,

chief god of the Greek pantheon,

decides to teach the inhabitants of Atlantis a lesson for their

avarice and prideful desire to rule the world.

Zeus gathers the gods together to relate his plan and

the dialogue ends.

In an earth-shattering upheaval far beyond our modern

understanding of catastrophe,

this beautiful land and its people were destroyed

in a day and a night.

Earthquakes, volcanic eruptions, and tidal waves,

with forces never before or since been allowed to run free by

nature, shattered the precious crystal towers,

sunk the great armada,

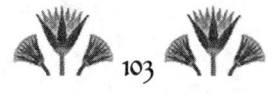

and created a upheaval of inestimable sorrow.

All that remains are the traces of those derivative cultures

that benefited from contact with

the most spectacular source of all culture.

But ancient Egypt, the Aztecs, the Maya,

the Chinese Shang, the Moundbuilders, and the rest,

as impressive as they are,

could have only been the faintest of shadows,

the most aimless of imitations of the source of all human

civilization.

For the original civilization of which I speak,

the source of all human achievement,

is Atlantis,

the island continent civilization that was obliterated beneath

the seething waters of the Atlantic more than eleven

thousand years ago...or did it?

Unlike many legends,

104

the source of the Atlantis story is quite easy to trace.

It all started with the Greek philosopher Plato.

Plato believed that the best way to instruct his students was
to embrace them in dialogues.

Plato wrote many of his philosophical treatises in a dialogue
format as well.

Readers who insist that the entire Atlantean dialogues are
genuine history may be uninformed that even the context of
Plato's dialogues is fictitious.

The dialogues were mainly imaginary conversations
between Socrates, Plato and his students.

The actual discussions Plato reported on never really
took place;

the published dialogues were not simply stenographic records.

It was simply a technique to challenge, teach and entertain
his students.

Critias says that he heard this 'true' story from his grandfather,

who related it at a public gathering on a holiday

that Plato scholar Paul Friedlander

refers to as a kind of April Fools Day when prizes were

awarded for the best narrative.

Critia's grandfather, also named Critias,

said that he heard it from his father, Dropides,

who heard it from the Greek sage Solon,

who heard it from some unnamed priests in Egypt when he

was there shortly after 600 BC. So, at best,

the Critias account of Atlantis is a very indirect account

of a story that originated more than two hundred years

earlier."[1]

—Kenneth L. Feder, Frauds Myths and
Mysteries: Science and Pseudoscience in Archaeology

"The Atlanteans were really the first purely human and
terrestrial race –
those that preceded it being more divine and ethereal
than human and solid.
Immense periods of time must have elapsed
since the separation of the sexes,
without mentioning the First or even the Second Root
Races.
As these must remain beyond the comprehension of minds
trained in Western thought,
it is found useless to speak in detail of the First and Second,
and even of the Third Race in its earliest stage.
One has to begin with the latter,
when it reached its full human period."[2]

—Helena P. Blavatsky
The Races of Man: Rounds and Races

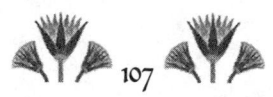

"The fifth seal represents the Atlantean cycle.

The vision of the souls beneath the altar is symbolical of the

Lemurians,

who were imprisoned in the space from where the moon was

born.

The ninth verse should read,

'and when he opened the fifth seal, I saw underneath the

altar the souls of them that had been slain

by the Word of God,

for their testimony, or belief, which they held.'

This shows a somewhat different light on the passage;

the altar beneath which they were imprisoned was the altar

where the Thothians were given material bodies

by the blood sacrifice,

a passage opening from beneath it

to the great space below.

The Lemurians were imprisoned there,

beneath the altar,

dead to the outer world,

by the power of the Word....

The moon like blood and the falling of stars are symbolical

of the great strife and unrest that took place among the

barbarous tribes after Atlantis sank.

When Altantis,

the Sun-kingdom, was destroyed,

the Atlantean governors,

who had established colonies among the barbarians,

were overthrown and cast down.

When the sun was darkened,

the power or energy which lighted the stars was no longer

present,

and so the stars, or rulers,

who depended upon the power of Atlantis for backing,

were cast down.

Heaven was removed,

the literal focal point of the full power of the Cosmic was

removed from earth's surface,

and the mountains were moved and changed,

and Shamballa formed beneath certain mountains in the high

Himalayas."[3]

—Dr. Doreal

Interpretation of the Book of Revelation

6:9-11 – 6:12-17

Perchance the most legendary account of a civilization being overcome by a watery catastrophe can be found in Plato's description of the destiny of Atlantis around 10,000 BC. This is only a fragment of the original document, translated by Benjamin Jowett.

"Let me begin by observing first of all, that nine thousand was the sum of years which had elapsed since the war which was said to have taken place between those who dwelt outside the

Pillars of Heracles

and all who dwelt within them; this war I am going to describe. Of the combatants on the one side, the city of Athens was reported to have been the leader and to have fought out the war; the combatants on the other side were commanded by

the kings of Atlantis,

which, as was saying,

was an island greater in extent than Libya and Asia,

and when afterwards sunk by an earthquake,

became an impassable barrier of mud to voyagers sailing from

hence to any part of the ocean.

The progress of the history will unfold the various nations

of barbarians and families of Hellenes which then existed,

as they successively appear on the scene;

but I must describe first of all Athenians of that day,

and their enemies who fought with them,

and then the respective powers and governments of the two

kingdoms.

Let us give the precedence to Athens.

In the days of old the gods had the whole earth distributed

among them by allotment. There was no quarrelling;

for you cannot rightly suppose that the gods did not know

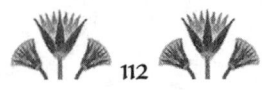

What was proper for each of them to have,

or, knowing this,

that they would seek to procure for themselves

by contention that which more properly

belonged to others.

They all of them by just apportionment obtained what they

wanted,

and peopled their own districts;

and when they had peopled them they tended us,

their nurselings and possessions,

as shepherds tend their flocks,

excepting only that they did not use blows or bodily force,

as shepherds do,

but governed us like pilots

from the stern of the vessel,

which is an easy way of guiding animals,

holding our souls by the rudder of persuasion according to

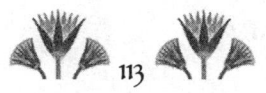

their own pleasure;

thus did they guide all mortal creatures.

Now different gods had their allotments in different places

which they set in order.

Hephaestus and Athene,

who were brother and sister,

and sprang from the same father,

having a common nature,

and being united also in the love of philosophy and art,

both obtained as their common portion this land,

which was naturally adapted for wisdom and virtue;

and there they implanted brave children of the soil,

and put into their minds the order of government;

their names are preserved,

but their actions have disappeared by reason of the destruction

of those who received the tradition,

and the lapse of ages.

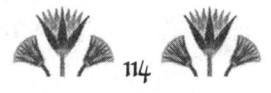

For when there were any survivors,

as I have already said,

they were men who dwelt in the mountains;

and they were ignorant of the art of writing,

and had heard only the names of the chiefs of the land,

but very little about their actions.

The names they were willing enough to give to their

children;

but the virtues and the laws of their predecessors,

they knew only by obscure traditions;

and as they themselves and their children lacked for many

generations the necessaries of life,

they directed their attention to the supply of their wants,

and of them they conversed,

to the neglect of events that had happened in times long past;

for mythology and the enquiry into antiquity are first

introduced into cities when they begin to have leisure,

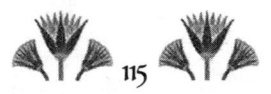

and when they see that the necessaries of life have already

been provided, but not before.

And this is reason why the names of the ancients have been

preserved to us and not their actions.

This I infer because Solon said that the priests in their

narrative of that war mentioned most of the names which are

recorded prior to the time of Theseus,

such as Cecrops,

and Erechtheus,

and Erichthonius,

and Erysichthon,

and the names of the women in like manner.

Moreover, since military pursuits were then common to men

and women,

the men of those days in accordance with the custom of the

time

set up a figure and image of the goddess in full armour,

to be a testimony that all animals which associate together,

male as well as female,

may, if they please,

practise in common the virtue which belongs to them without

distinction of sex.

Now the country was inhabited in those days by various

classes of citizens;

there were artisans,

and there were husbandmen,

and there was also a warrior class originally set apart

by divine men.

The latter dwelt by themselves,

and had all things suitable for nurture and education;

neither had any of them anything of their own,

but they regarded all that they had as common property;

nor did they claim to receive of the other citizens anything

more than their necessary food.

And they practised all the pursuits which we yesterday

described as those of our imaginary guardians.

Concerning the country the Egyptian priests said what is

not only probable but manifestly true,

that the boundaries were in those days fixed by the Isthmus,

and that in the direction of the continent they extended as far

as the heights of Cithaeron and Parnes;

the boundary line came down in the direction of the sea,

having the district of Oropus on the right,

and with the river Asopus as the limit on the left.

The land was the best in the world,

and was therefore able in those days to support a vast army,

raised from the surrounding people.

Even the remnant of Attica which now exists

may compare with any region in the world for the

variety and excellence

of its fruits and the suitableness of its pastures to every

sort of animal,

which proves what I am saying;

but in those days the country was fair as now and yielded far

more abundant produce.

How shall I establish my words? and what part of it can

be truly called a remnant of the land that then was?

The whole country is only a long promontory extending far

into the sea away from the rest of the continent,

while the surrounding basin of the sea is everywhere deep in

the neighbourhood of the shore.

Many great deluges have taken place during the

nine thousand years,

for that is the number of years which have elapsed since the

time of which I am speaking;

and during all this time and through so many changes,

there has never been any considerable accumulation of the soil

coming down from the mountains,

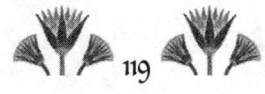

as in other places, but the earth has fallen away all round

and sunk out of sight.

The consequence is,

that in comparison of what then was,

there are remaining only the bones of the wasted body,

as they may be called,

as in the case of small islands,

all the richer and softer parts of the soil having fallen away,

and the mere skeleton of the land being left.

But in the primitive state of the country,

its mountains were high hills covered with soil, and the plains,

as they are termed by us,

of Phelleus were full of rich earth,

and there was abundance of wood in the mountains.

Of this last the traces still remain,

for although some of the mountains now only afford

sustenance to bees,

not so very long ago there were still to be seen roofs

of timber cut from trees growing there,

which were of a size sufficient to cover the largest houses;

and there were many other high trees,

cultivated by man and bearing abundance of food for cattle.

Moreover, the land reaped the benefit of the annual

rainfall, not as now losing the water which flows off the bare

earth into the sea, but,

having an abundant supply in all places,

and receiving it into herself and treasuring it up in the

close clay soil,

it let off into the hollows the streams which it absorbed from

the heights,

providing everywhere abundant fountains and rivers,

of which there may still be observed sacred memorials in

places where fountains once existed;

and this proves the truth of what I am saying.

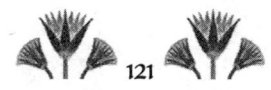

Such was the natural state of the country,

which was cultivated, as we may well believe,

by true husbandmen, who made husbandry their business,

and were lovers of honour,

and of a noble nature,

and had a soil the best in the world,

and abundance of water,

and in the heaven above an excellently attempered climate.

Now the city in those days was arranged on this wise.

In the first place the Acropolis was not as now.

For the fact is that a single night of excessive rain washed

away the earth and laid bare the rock;

at the same time there were earthquakes,

and then occurred the extraordinary inundation,

which was the third before the great destruction of

Deucalion.

But in primitive times the hill of the Acropolis extended to

the Eridanus and Ilissus,

and included the Pnyx on one side,

and the Lycabettus as a boundary on the opposite side

to the Pnyx,

and was all well covered with soil, and level at the top,

except in one or two places.

Outside the Acropolis

and under the sides of the hill there dwelt artisans,

and such of the husbandmen as were tilling the ground near;

the warrior class dwelt by themselves around the

temples of Athene and Hephaestus at the summit,

which moreover they had enclosed with a single fence like the

garden of a single house.

On the north side they had dwellings in common and had

erected halls for dining in winter,

and had all the buildings which they needed

for their common life, besides temples,

but there was no adorning of them with gold and silver,

for they made no use of these for any purpose;

they took a middle course between meanness and ostentation,

and built modest houses in which they and their childrens'

children grew old,

and they handed them down to others who were like

themselves,

always the same.

But in summer-time they left their gardens and gymnasia

and dining halls,

and then the southern side of the hill was made use of by them

for the same purpose.

Where the Acropolis now is there was a fountain,

which was choked by the earthquake,

and has left only the few small streams which still

exist in the vicinity,

but in those days the fountain gave an abundant supply of

Water for all and of suitable temperature in summer and in
winter.

This is how they dwelt,

being the guardians of their own citizens and the leaders of the
Hellenes, who were their willing followers.

And they took care to preserve the same number of men and
women through all time,

being so many as were required

for warlike purposes,

then as now-that is to say,

about twenty thousand.

Such were the ancient Athenians,

and after this manner they righteously administered their own
land and the rest of Hellas;

they were renowned all over Europe and Asia for the

beauty of their persons and for the many virtues of their souls,

and of all men who lived in those days they were the most

illustrious.

And next, if I have not forgotten what I heard when
I was a child,
I will impart to you the character and origin of their
adversaries.
For friends should not keep their stories to themselves,
but have them in common.
Yet, before proceeding further in the narrative,
I ought to warn you, that you must not be surprised if you
should perhaps hear Hellenic names given to foreigners.
I will tell you the reason of this: Solon,
who was intending to use the tale for his poem,
enquired into the meaning of the names,
and found that the early Egyptians in writing them down
had translated them into their own language,
and he recovered the meaning of the several names and when
copying them out again translated them into our language.

My great-grandfather, Dropides,

had the original writing, which is still in my possession,

and was carefully studied by me when I was a child.

Therefore if you hear names such as are used in this

country,

you must not be surprised,

for I have told how they came to be introduced.

The tale,

which was of great length, began as follows:

I have before remarked in speaking of the allotments of the

gods,

that they distributed the whole earth into portions differing in

extent,

and made for themselves temples and instituted sacrifices.

And Poseidon,

receiving for his lot the island of Atlantis,

begat children by a mortal woman,

and settled them in a part of the island,

which I will describe.

Looking towards the sea,

but in the centre of the whole island,

there was a plain which is said to have been the fairest of all

plains and very fertile.

Near the plain again,

and also in the centre of the island

at a distance of about fifty stadia,

there was a mountain not very high on any side.

In this mountain there dwelt one of the earth born primeval

men of that country,

whose name was Evenor,

and he had a wife named Leucippe,

and they had an only daughter who was called Cleito.

The maiden had already reached womanhood,

When her father and mother died;

Poseidon fell in love with her and had intercourse with her,

and breaking the ground,

inclosed the hill in which she dwelt all round,

making alternate zones of sea and land larger and smaller,

encircling one another;

there were two of land and three of water,

which he turned as with a lathe,

each having its circumference equidistant every way from the

centre,

so that no man could get to the island,

for ships and voyages were not as yet.

He himself, being a god,

found no difficulty in making special arrangements

for the centre island,

bringing up two springs of water from beneath the earth,

one of warm water and the other of cold,

and making every variety of food to spring up abundantly

from the soil.

He also begat and brought up five pairs of twin male

children;

and dividing the island of Atlantis into ten portions,

he gave to the first-born of the eldest pair his mother's

dwelling and the surrounding allotment,

which was the largest and best,

and made him king over the rest;

the others he made princes,

and gave them rule over many men, and a large territory.

And he named them all;

the eldest, who was the first king,

he named Atlas,

and after him the whole island and the ocean were called

Atlantic.

To his twin brother, who was born after him,

130

and obtained as his lot the extremity of the island towards the

Pillars of Heracles,

facing the country which is now called

the region of Gades

in that part of the world,

he gave the name which in the Hellenic language is

Eumelus,

in the language of the country which is named after him,

Gadeirus.

Of the second pair of twins he called one Ampheres,

and the other Evaemon.

To the elder of the third pair of twins he gave the name

Mneseus, and Autochthon

to the one who followed him.

Of the fourth pair of twins he called the elder Elasippus,

and the younger Mestor.

And of the fifth pair he gave to the elder the name of

Azaes,

and to the younger that of Diaprepes.

All these and their descendants for many generations were

the inhabitants and rulers of divers islands in the open sea;

and also, as has been already said,

they held sway in our direction over the country within the

Pillars as far as Egypt and Tyrrhenia.

Now Atlas had a numerous and honourable family,

and they retained the kingdom,

the eldest son handing it on to his eldest for many generations;

and they had such an amount of wealth as was never before

possessed by kings and potentates,

and is not likely ever to be again,

and they were furnished with everything which they needed,

both in the city and country.

For because of the greatness of their empire many things

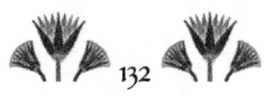

were brought to them from foreign countries,

and the island itself provided most of what was required by

them for the uses of life.

In the first place, they dug out of the earth

whatever was to be found there,

solid as well as fusile,

and that which is now only a name and was then

something more than a name,

orichalcum,

was dug out of the earth in many parts of the island,

being more precious in those days than anything except gold.

There was an abundance of wood for carpenter's work,

and sufficient maintenance for tame and wild animals.

Moreover, there were a great number of elephants in the

island;

for as there was provision for all other sorts of animals,

both for those which live in lakes and marshes and rivers,

and also for those which live in mountains and on plains,

so there was for the animal which is the largest and most

voracious of all.

Also whatever fragrant things there now are in the earth,

whether roots,

or herbage, or woods, or essences which distil from fruit and

flower,

grew and thrived in that land;

also the fruit which admits of cultivation,

both the dry sort,

which is given us for nourishment and any other which we use

for food - we call them all by the common

name pulse, and the fruits having a hard rind,

affording drinks and meats and ointments,

and good store of chestnuts and the like,

which furnish pleasure and amusement,

and are fruits which spoil with keeping,

and the pleasant kinds of dessert,

with which we console ourselves after dinner,

when we are tired of eating - all these that sacred island

which then beheld the light of the sun,

brought forth fair and wondrous and in infinite abundance.

With such blessings the earth freely furnished them;

meanwhile they went on constructing their temples and palaces

and harbours and docks.

And they arranged the whole country in the following

manner:

First of all they bridged over the zones of sea which

surrounded the ancient metropolis,

making a road to and from the royal palace.

And at the very beginning they built the palace

in the habitation of the god and of their ancestors,

which they continued to ornament in successive generations,

every king surpassing the one who went before him to the

utmost of his power,

until they made the building a marvel to behold for size and

for beauty.

And beginning from the sea they bored a canal of three

hundred feet in width and one hundred feet in depth and fifty

stadia in length,

which they carried through to the outermost zone,

making a passage from the sea up to this,

which became a harbour,

and leaving an opening sufficient to enable the largest vessels

to find ingress.

Moreover, they divided at the bridges the zones of land

which parted the zones of sea,

leaving room for a single trireme to pass out of one zone into

another,

and they covered over the channels so as to leave a way

underneath for the ships;

for the banks were raised considerably above the water.

Now the largest of the zones into which a passage was cut

from the sea was three stadia in breadth,

and the zone of land which came next of equal breadth;

but the next two zones, the one of water,

the other of land, were two stadia,

and the one which surrounded the central island

was a stadium only in width.

The island in which the palace was situated had a diameter

of five stadia.

All this including the zones and the bridge,

which was the sixth part of a stadium in width,

they surrounded by a stone wall on every side,

placing towers and gates on the bridges where the sea

passed in.

The stone which was used in the work they quarried from

underneath the centre island,

and from underneath the zones,

on the outer as well as the inner side.

One kind was white, another black,

and a third red, and as they quarried,

they at the same time hollowed out double docks, having roofs

formed out of the native rock.

Some of their buildings were simple,

but in others they put together different stones,

varying the colour to please the eye,

and to be a natural source of delight.

The entire circuit of the wall,

which went round the outermost zone,

they covered with a coating of brass,

and the circuit of the next wall they coated with tin,

and the third, which encompassed the citadel,

flashed with the red light of orichalcum.

The palaces in the interior of the citadel were constructed

on this wise:

in the centre was a holy temple dedicated to Cleito and
Poseidon,

which remained inaccessible,

and was surrounded by an enclosure of gold;

this was the spot where the family of the ten princes first saw
the light,

and thither the people annually brought

the fruits of the earth in their season from all the ten portions,

to be an offering to each of the ten.

Here was Poseidon's own temple which was

a stadium in length,

and half a stadium in width, and of a proportionate height,

having a strange barbaric appearance.

All the outside of the temple,

with the exception of the pinnacles, they covered with silver,

and the pinnacles with gold.

In the interior of the temple the roof was of ivory,

curiously wrought everywhere with gold and silver and

orichalcum;

and all the other parts, the walls and pillars and floor,

they coated with orichalcum.

In the temple they placed statues of gold:

there was the god himself standing in a chariot

– the charioteer of six winged horses –

and of such a size that he touched the roof of the building

with his head;

around him there were a hundred Nereids riding on dolphins,

for such was thought to be the number of them by the

men of those days.

There were also in the interior of the temple other images

which had been dedicated by private persons.

And around the temple on the outside were placed statues of

gold of all the descendants of the ten kings and of their wives,

and there were many other great offerings of kings and of

private persons,

coming both from the city itself and from the foreign cities

over which they held sway.

There was an altar too,

which in size and workmanship corresponded to this

magnificence,

and the palaces, in like manner,

answered to the greatness of the kingdom

and the glory of the temple.

In the next place,

they had fountains,

one of cold and another of hot water,

in gracious plenty flowing;

and they were wonderfully

adapted for use by reason of the pleasantness and excellence

of their waters.

They constructed buildings about them and planted suitable

trees, also they made cisterns, some open to the heavens,

others roofed over, to be used in winter as warm baths;

there were the kings baths, and the baths of private persons,

which were kept apart;

and there were separate baths for women,

and for horses and cattle, and to each of them they gave as

much adornment as was suitable.

Of the water which ran off they carried some to the grove

of Poseidon,

where were growing all manner of trees of wonderful height

and beauty, owing to the excellence of the soil,

while the remainder was conveyed by aqueducts along the

bridges to the outer circles;

and there were many temples built and dedicated to many

gods;

also gardens and places of exercise,

some for men, and others for horses in both of

the two islands formed by the zones;

and in the centre of the larger

of the two there was set apart a race-course of a stadium in

width,

and in length allowed to extend all round the island,

for horses to race in.

Also there were guardhouses at intervals for the guards,

the more trusted of whom were appointed,

to keep watch in the lesser zone,

which was nearer the Acropolis

while the most trusted of all had houses given them

within the citadel,

near the persons of the kings.

The docks were full of triremes and naval stores,

and all things were quite ready for use.

Enough of the plan of the royal palace.

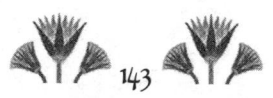

Leaving the palace and passing out across the three you

came to a wall which began at the sea and went all round:

this was everywhere distant fifty stadia from the largest zone

or harbour, and enclosed the whole,

the ends meeting at the mouth of the channel

which led to the sea.

The entire area was densely crowded with habitations;

and the canal and the largest of the harbours were full of

vessels and merchants coming from all parts,

who, from their numbers,

kept up a multitudinous sound of human voices,

and din and clatter of all sorts night and day.

I have described the city and the environs of the ancient

palace nearly in the words of Solon,

and now I must endeavour to represent the nature and

arrangement of the rest of the land.

The whole country was said by him to be very lofty and

precipitous on the side of the sea,

but the country immediately about and surrounding the city

was a level plain,

itself surrounded by mountains which descended towards the

sea;

it was smooth and even, and of an oblong shape,

extending in one direction three thousand stadia,

but across the centre inland it was two thousand stadia.

This part of the island looked towards the south,

and was sheltered from the north.

The surrounding mountains were celebrated for their

number and size and beauty, far beyond any which still exist,

having in them also many wealthy villages of country folk,

and rivers, and lakes, and meadows supplying food enough for

every animal, wild or tame, and much wood of various sorts,

abundant for each and every kind of work.

I will now describe the plain,

as it was fashioned by nature and by the labours of many

generations of kings through long ages.

It was for the most part rectangular and oblong,

and where falling out of the straight line followed the

circular ditch.

The depth, and width, and length of this ditch were

incredible,

and gave the impression that a work of such extent,

in addition to so many others,

could never have been artificial.

Nevertheless I must say what I was told.

It was excavated to the depth of a hundred feet,

and its breadth was a stadium everywhere;

it was carried round the whole of the plain,

and was ten thousand stadia in length.

It received the streams which came down from the mountains,

and winding round the plain and meeting at the city,

was there let off into the sea.

Further inland, likewise,

straight canals of a hundred feet in width were cut from it

through the plain,

and again let off into the ditch leading to the sea:

these canals were at intervals of a hundred stadia,

and by them they brought down the wood from the mountains

to the city,

and conveyed the fruits of the earth in ships, cutting transverse

passages from one canal into another,

and to the city.

Twice in the year they gathered the fruits of the earth

in winter having the benefit of the rains of heaven,

and in summer the water which the land supplied by

introducing streams from the canals.

As to the population, each of the lots in the plain had to

find a leader for the men who were fit for military service,

and the size of a lot was a square of ten stadia each way,

and the total number of all the lots was

sixty thousand.

And of the inhabitants of the mountains and of the rest of

the country there was also a vast multitude,

which was distributed among the lots and had leaders assigned

to them according to their districts and villages.

The leader was required to furnish for the war

the sixth portion of a war-chariot,

so as to make up a total of ten thousand chariots;

also two horses and riders for them,

and a pair of chariot-horses without a seat,

accompanied by a horseman who could fight on foot carrying

a small shield,

and having a charioteer who stood behind the man-at-arms to

guide the two horses; also, he was bound to furnish two heavy

armed soldiers, two slingers,

three stone-shooters

and three javelin-men, who were light-armed,

and four sailors to make up the complement of twelve hundred

ships.

Such was the military order of the royal city,

the order of the other nine governments varied,

and it would be wearisome to recount their several differences.

As to offices and honours,

the following was the arrangement from the first.

Each of the ten kings in his own division and in his own city

had the absolute control of the citizens, and, in most cases,

of the laws, punishing and slaying whomsoever he would.

Now the order of precedence among them and their mutual

relations were regulated by the commands of Poseidon

which the law had handed down.

These were inscribed by the first kings on a pillar of

orichalcum,

which was situated in the middle of the island,

at the temple of Poseidon,

whither the kings were gathered together every fifth and

every sixth year alternately,

thus giving equal honour to the odd and to the even number.

And when they were gathered together they consulted about

their common interests,

and enquired if any one had transgressed in anything and

passed judgment and before they passed judgment they gave

their pledges to one another on this wise:

There were bulls who had the range of the temple of

Poseidon;

and the ten kings, being left alone in the temple,

after they had offered prayers to the god that they might

capture the victim which was acceptable to him,

hunted the bulls,

without weapons but with staves and nooses;

and the bull which they caught they led up to the pillar and

cut its throat over the top of it so that the blood fell upon the

sacred inscription.

Now on the pillar, besides the laws,

there was inscribed an oath invoking mighty curses on the

disobedient.

When therefore, after slaying the bull in the accustomed

manner, they had burnt its limbs, they filled a bowl of wine

and cast in a clot of blood for each of them;

the rest of the victim they put in the fire,

after having purified the column all round.

Then they drew from the bowl in golden cups and pouring a

libation on the fire,

they swore that they would judge according to the laws

on the pillar, and would punish him who in any point had

already transgressed them,

151

and that for the future they would not,

if they could help,

offend against the writing on the pillar,

and would neither command others, nor obey any ruler who

commanded them, to act otherwise than according

to the laws of their father Poseidon.

This was the prayer which each of them offered up

for himself and for his descendants,

at the same time drinking and dedicating the cup out of which

he drank in the temple of the god;

and after they had supped and satisfied their needs,

when darkness came on, and the fire about the sacrifice was

cool,

all of them put on most beautiful azure robes, and,

sitting on the ground, at night,

over the embers of the sacrifices by which they had sworn,

and extinguishing all the fire about the temple,

they received and gave judgment,

if any of them had an accusation to bring against any one;

and when they given judgment,

at daybreak they wrote down their sentences on a golden

tablet,

and dedicated it together with their robes to be a memorial.
There were many special laws affecting the several kings

inscribed about the temples,

but the most important was the following:
They were not to take up arms against one another,

and they were all to come to the rescue if any one in any of

their cities attempted to overthrow the royal house;

like their ancestors,

they were to deliberate in common about war and other

matters,

giving the supremacy to the descendants of Atlas.
And the king was not to have the power of life and death

over any of his kinsmen unless he had the assent of the

majority of the ten.

Such was the vast power which the god settled in the lost

island of Atlantis;

and this he afterwards directed against our land for

the following reasons,

as tradition tells:

For many generations,

as long as the divine nature lasted in them,

they were obedient to the laws,

and well-affectioned towards the god,

whose seed they were;

for they possessed true and in every way great spirits,

uniting gentleness with wisdom in the various chances of life,

and in their intercourse with one another.

They despised everything but virtue,

caring little for their present state of life,

and thinking lightly of the possession of gold and other

property,

which seemed only a burden to them;

neither were they intoxicated by luxury;

nor did wealth deprive them of their self-control;

but they were sober,

and saw clearly that all these goods are increased by virtue

and friendship with one another,

whereas by too great regard and respect for them,

they are lost and friendship with them.

By such reflections and by the continuance in them of a

divine nature,

the qualities which we have described grew and increased

among them;

but when the divine portion began to fade away,

and became diluted too often and too much with the mortal

admixture, and the human nature got the upper hand,

they then, being unable to bear their fortune,

behaved unseemly,

and to him who had an eye to see grew visibly debased,

for they were losing the fairest of their precious gifts;

but to those who had no eye to see the true happiness,

they appeared glorious and blessed at the very time when they

were full of avarice and unrighteous power.

Zeus, the god of gods,

who rules according to law, and is able to see into such things,

perceiving that an honourable race was in a woeful plight,

and wanting to inflict punishment on them,

that they might be chastened and improve,

collected all the gods into their most holy habitation, which,

being placed in the centre of the world,

beholds all created things.

And when he had called them together,

he spake as follows..."[4]

The rest of the dialogue of Critias was either never completed or has been lost over time....

—Plato, Critias

"Atlantis...the Great empire which sank in one night,

flooding the world...

The fabled land of Atlantis,

as it was called by Iberian Greeks.

Called Atlakika by Basques,

Avalon by the Irish Celtics and

Atli by the Vikings."[5]

—Ignatius Donnelly

The Antediluvian World: The History of

Atlantis 1882

"Eleven thousand years ago,
the water level of the ocean was perhaps three hundred feet
lower than it is today.
When the Ice Age ended,
billions of gallons of ice and snow melted into the sea,
resulting in a dramatic,
sudden,
and terrifying rising of the sea level all around the world.
The eastern coastline of the United States was some one
hundred miles farther out in the Atlantic Ocean during
the Ice Age.
The rise of water undoubtedly caused the flooding of many
low-level seaside communities.
If the rising of the sea level was so sudden that it caused the
flooding and disappearance of towns and cities in coastal
areas,
it could have also caused a large,

low-lying island to similarly be swallowed up by the higher level of the ocean, leaving only the tops of its highest sections visible; just as legend describes.

'Atlantis,

as the land was called by seafaring people,

was swallowed by the waves together with its mountains

and valleys,

and everything else was covered by the sea.

Many people were buried in the ground and others,

who escaped,

died in the water.'"[6]

—A. G. Galanopoulos
Atlantis: The truth behind the legend

"In Cape Sunium,

the nearest point on the Greek mainland to Thera,

there is a story of a legendary contest for the possession of Attica,

part of Thera Proper between Athena and Poseidon.

According to the legend,

Athena and Poseidon each produced a gift for the people of Attica.

Athena produced and olive tree,

and Poseidon a spring.

Athena's gift was judged the more useful,

and Poseidon lost.

Poseidon was a bad loser: and in his anger,

he flooded the country.

Poseidon was very wrathful,

and flooded the Therasian plain round Eleusis,

and submerged Attica under sea-water....

The volcano obliterated settlements on Thera and
wrecked the island,
and what it did to Thera may still be seen and
studied in detail,
and forms the strongest testimony to the destructiveness
of the eruption."[7]

J. V. Luce
Lost Atlantis: new light on an old legend

"Creative powers in man were the gift of divine wisdom,

not the result of sin.

The curse was not brought on mankind by the Fourth

Race,

for the comparatively sinless Third Race,

the still more gigantic Antediluvians,

had perished in the same way;

hence the Deluge was no punishment,

but simply a result of a periodical and geological law.

The secret teachings show that

the Deluge overtook the Fourth, giant Race,

not on account of their depravity,

or because they had become black with sin,

but simply because such is the fate of every continent,

which - like everything else under our Sun -

is born, lives, becomes decrepit, and dies.

This was when the Fifth Race was in its infancy.

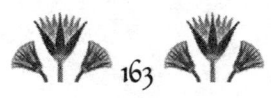

A decree had come indeed;

the decree of nature and the Law of Evolution,

that the earth should change its race,

and that the Fourth Race should be destroyed

to make room for a better one.

The Manvantara had reached its turning point of three

and a half Rounds,

and gigantic physical Humanity had reached the acme of

gross materiality."[8]

—Helena P. Blavatsky
The Races of Man: The Atlanteans

164

Here Edgar Cayce, the distinguished American healer and visionary, reinforces the reality of both Atlantis and of its eventual destruction by flood in around 10,000[i] years BC, following the same abuse of technical powers no less compelling and highly developed than our own technologies of today.

The following Readings by Edgar Cayce, tape recorded while in a sleep-induced trance, describe the conflict of the Sons of the Law of One, the patriarchs of Atlantis, and Son Belial and later, the Sons of Belial, who brought about the final destruction to Poseidia by the misapplication of spiritual laws in material ways and manners.

---

[i] A period acknowledged geologically to have marked an especially rapid rise in world sea levels.

Reading: 263-4

"The entity was in the Atlantean land,

in those periods when there first began the with drawings

from the Law of One,

those establishings of the sons –

or of the Son Belial in that experience."

Reading: 339-1

"The entity was in the Atlantean period when there were

those contentions between those of the one faith

and those that were of Bel-Ra – or the idol worshippers.

In the household of the king

before the third destruction."

Reading: 378-13

"In Atlantis we find the entity,

166

as there were those periods before the destruction –

when there were being continually waged what may be termed

war, but rather in the sense as would be considered in the

present period when there is being a campaign by individuals

or groups respecting the impulsive influence that is directing

the activities of the man, the brother, the neighbor, the

associate.

Or, as would be termed, an evangelistic campaign.

This was being waged between the followers

of the patriarchs of old;

of Alta, of Quoauda,

and those that directed against the sons of Baalilal."

Reading: 390-2

"Entity was in the Atlantean period before the

second of the turmoils that separated the islands

or broke up the land into islands;

and in the city of Eden

in Poseidia did the entity then dwell.

The entity was among the Atlan lands

and peoples and of those that served in the temple

during the building of the temple to the One,

the law of the One,

the understanding of the law of the One.

Then the entity became enamored

with those of the house of Baalilal,

and faltered in the experience;

yet it was forgiven much through those sojournings in the

understandings

of that given through Quoauda in the land."

Reading: 416-1

"Entity was in that land known as the Atlantean,

during those periods when there was

168

the second of the destructive forces

that brought destruction to those both of the

one faith and those of Baalilal."

Reading: 470-22

"As indicated from that just given,

the entity was in Atlantis when there was the

second period of disturbance –

which would be some twenty-two thousand, five hundred

22,500 years before the periods of the Egyptian activity

covered by the Exodus;

or it was some twenty-eight thousand 28,000 years

before Christ.

Then we had a period where the activities in the

Atlantean land became more in provinces,

or there were small channels through many of the lands.

And there were those,

with the entity and its associates or companions, who left the

activities to engage in the building

up of the activities in the Peruvian land.

For the Atlanteans were becoming decadent,

or being broken up owing to the disputes between

the children of the Law of One

and the children of Belial."

Reading: 1003-2

"Entity was in the Atlantean period.

Entity made those choices

for the Sons of the Law of One,

and when the entity had to make those choices for that

as was to deal with those who brought destruction

by the misapplication of spiritual laws

in material ways and manners.

Those as we find were the periods when the entity excelled

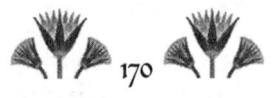

in those things that had to do with machinery,

mechanics,

the application of electrical forces

as would be called today those of radiation,

and heating,

and the applications of same to the uses for crafts,

for homes,

for buildings,

the use of same in the associations of what would be called

today commercial ways and manners."

Reading: 1023-2

"Entity was in the land now called the Atlantean,

during those periods when –

before the destructive forces that arose in the land –

there were the particular activities in the communications;

not only by the lighter than air machines

but by the developments of the communications

in what are now known as

the radio-active forces.

Those were a portion of the entity's activity,

and in conjunction with those that supervised such associations

did the entity give and lend aid and counsel that made for the

establishing of such an influence of those in the land

during that sojourn.

The entity was among those who aided not only the lowly

but those in authority;

losing only in trying to defend some of the associations

against the activities of the children of Belial.

But there was developing throughout the experience."

Reading: 877-26

"Hence we find there had been the separating into groups

as we would call them for this or that phase of activity;

and those that were against that manner of development.
The Sons of Belial were of one group,
or those that sought more the gratifying, the satisfying,
the use of material things for self,
without thought or consideration as to the sources of such
nor the hardships in the experiences of others.
Or, in other words, as we would term it today,
they were those without a standard of morality.
The other group –
those who followed the Law of One – had a standard.
The Sons of Belial had no standard,
save of self,
self-aggrandizement."

Reading: 1968-1

"Before that the entity was in the Atlantean land,

during those periods of the first of the destructive forces.

There we find the entity was in a state of turmoil

because of the activities of the sons of Belial,

and with those of the daughters of the children of One.

For the entity had disputations,

being physically in love with one of the sons of Belial,

and yet giving in its service,

giving in its activities with

the children of the Law of One."

Reading: 2301-1

"The entity was among those who came to the Egyptian

land during periods of breaking up of the land,

of the children of the Law of One,

yet coveting the principles of the children of Belial;

174

thus causing in part those disturbances which arose in the
Egyptian period of the entity's activity there.
Hence with the associations of and others of that group who
undertook to hold to those activities which arose by
the banishment of the Priest,
the entity was only brought to the better understanding
with the return of the Priest,
through the aid from some of the Natives,
and a few of the entity's own people."

Reading: 2794-3
"As we have indicated,
the Atlanteans were those that had reached an advancement,
had been entrusted with divine activities in the earth,
and - as the entity - forgot from whom,
in whom all live and have their being;
thus brought about within themselves –

that which destroyed the body,

but not the soul."

Reading: 2795-1

"Entity was in the Atlantean land,

when there were those usages of the high developments

in the activities of the mechanical nature.

Thus the entity was one who builded the planes,

those activities in air, in water,

as directed by the stone [ii]

from which the forces were generated –

or such as the radio beam in the present,

from that central facet

for which the entity made those experiences –

and that are the dreams of the entity in the present.

These may be used for constructive or destructive forces.

[ii] Firestone, described as a crystal through which the sun's rays, or energy was magnified to create a laser ray through the crystal's prisms were connected to a mode of travel.

176

These were allowed to become, or did become,

those forces that brought about

the last breaking up of Poseidia.

In the experience the entity held fast to the creative purposes

but was overruled by the sons of Belial,

when those warrings began between

the sons of the children of the Law of One

and the sons of Belial."[9]

—Edgar Cayce
Readings. Continent and Culture of Atlantis

"The civilization of the Atlanteans was greater
even than that of the Egyptians.
It is their degenerate descendants, the nation of Plato's
Atlantis,
which built the first pyramids in the country,
and that certainly before the advent of the
'Eastern Ethiopians,'
as Herodotus called the Egyptians."[10]

—Helena P. Blavatsky
The Races of Man: The Atlanteans

178

"In the case of war the Atlanteans had more than one million soldiers. Ramses III claimed to have beaten hundreds of thousands of enemies...he spoke of millions and myriads of enemies who were numerous like locusts or grasshoppers. Atlantis consisted of ten countries, according to the Karnak inscription written under pharaoh Merenptah around 1200 BC, the Sea Peoples consisted of the Ekwesh, Teresh, Lukka, Sherden, and Shekelesh. According to Ramses III, their confederation consisted of the union of the countries of the Peleset, Theker, Shekelesh, Denen, and Weshesh."[11]

—Rainer W. Kühne, *The Location and Dating of Atlantis*

Fig. 4. Painting of the mythical harbor of Atlantis.

Chapter 3

Tales of Creation, Emanation & Evolution

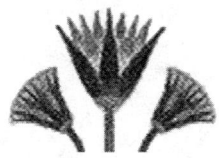

Fig. 5. Ur-Nippur Tablet. Sample of the "Flood Mud" discovered beneath Ur, and the Nippur Tablet, a clay tablet from ancient Nippur which is the only surviving document of the Sumerian flood story, dating from the 17th century BC. Written in Sumerian, it not only tells the flood story, but also describes the creation of humans and animals, and records the names of antediluvian cities and their rulers.

"It is a time for us to learn history,
it is time for the younger as well as the elder brother
to listen
to the history of the ancient ones."[1]

—Ramon Gil Barros
Message to the Younger Brother

"When looking around at the world
in which Man finds himself,
the silent query of his awakened consciousness is:
How did this grand aggregate of forms and Beings come
into existence?
Coupled with this query is another and more basic one:
Who and what am I,
the spectator, the thinker and the inquirer?
The Wisdom-Religion holds that these two questions
are inseparable, and that an answer to the one is contained
in the answer to the other.
The key to the mystery of Universal Being
is to be found in the knowledge by Man of Himself."[2]

—Helena P. Blavatsky
Theosophy Magazine

"Aum,

sacred symbol and infinite unheard Sound

which is the origin of all names and forms.

Aum is beyond description and predication,

objectification and duality:

Aum—this syllable is the whole world.

The past, the present, the future—

everything is just the word Aum.

And whatever else that transcends

threefold time— that too, is just the word Aum....

This is the Lord of all. This is the all-knowing.

This is the inner controller. This is the source of all,

for this is the origin and end of beings."[3]

—Swami Krishnananda

Mandukya Upanishad

"And Solomon was David's heir and he said,

'O men,

we have been taught the language of the birds

— ullimna mantiq at-tayr —

and all favors have been showered upon us.'"[4]

—Koran 27:15

"The language of the birds,

which can also be called 'angelic language'

and which is symbolized in the human world by rhythmic

language,

for the science of rhythm...

is in fact ultimately the basis of all the means that can be

brought into action in order to enter into communication with

the higher states of being.

This is why it is said in an Islamic tradition,

that Adam, while in the earthly paradise,

spoke in verse, that is,

in rhythmic language.

It is also why the Sacred Books are written

in rhythmic language."[5]

—René Guénon

The Language of the Birds

"The first to be born were the Kaggaba,

the Wiwa,

the Iku Kankuamos,

the Chimilas,

The Wayu,

and other native peoples.

Afterwards,

from the last semen were born the French,

the Germans,

Spaniards,

and people from faraway lands;

all of the younger brothers.

It was there,

in the Sierra Nevada de Santa Marta,

that the semen was studied,

and that is why it is the heart, the heart of everything.

We, the native people of Gonawindua,

were given the mission of looking after the heart of the

brothers alike.

Gonawindua,

the Sierra Nevada,

is the center of the universe...

this land is so sacred...

it is the heart of every heart.

In the old times, we had great wisdom,

given to us by Mother.

We had the knowledge of everything we were and are.

We knew, according to our law,

not to kill to many animals,

and not to cut down too many trees.

We knew what complies with the law bequeathed us.

The law was not written in books

but in our nature,

which is itself a book.

There have already been four histories of the world.

We are at the end of the fourth one.

In the first,

the waters came and filled the earth all the way up to the

sierra.

Everyone died.

Then came other peoples.

Their was evil, violence, and disrespect;

and when the violence grew too strong,

the sickness came,

and so the second world came to an end.

Afterwards,

in the next age,

the sun raised its heat, but not everyone died.

Then the sun went dark,

and although there was some light,

there was no warmth.

Still there were survivors.

It was then that an evil spirit came,

and his name was Petiku Umabash Umahuaba.

He would bite the people the way you bite a ripe,

yellow plantain,

and so it was that he finished them off.

The world ended for a third time.

Harm is being done to the land.

Nature is no longer the Mother:

it is something to be sold...

harmony, traditional thought,

and compliance with

Mother and Father have been lost."[6]

—Ramon Gil Barros
Message to the Younger Brother

"In matters of faith,

and in order to know the truth,

the hearing is superior to vision.

You must know that the Holy Spirit,

in order to cause a soul to advance in spirituality

educates the hearing before coming to the vision.

'Listen, holy child,' he says, 'and see.'

Why do you strain to see?

It is necessary to lend the ear.

The hearing, moreover, will restore vision to us,

if our attention is pious, faithful and vigilant.

Only the hearing attains to truth

because it perceives the verb —Word.

And thus one must awaken the hearing and train it

to receive the truth."[7]

—Saint Bernard of Clairvaux

"*What things soever ye desire,*

when ye pray,

believe that ye receive them,

and ye shall have them."[8]

— *Mark 11:24*

"There is no remembrance of former things;

neither shall there be any remembrance of things

that are to come

with those that shall come after."[9]

–King Solomon
Ecclesiastes 11

"Enki made his voice heard...

Dismantle the house, build a boat

Reject possessions, and save living things.

The boat that you build...

make upper and lower decks.

The tackle must be very strong,

the bitumen strong,

to give it strength.

I shall make rain fall on you here.

The Flood roared like a bull,

Like a wild ass screaming the winds

The darkness was total, there was no sun...

For seven days and seven nights

The torrent, storm and flood came on...."[10]

—Akkadian version of *The Story of Atrahasis*

"For six days and seven nights the wind blew,

flood and tempest overwhelmed the land;

When the seventh day arrived the tempest,

flood and onslaught which had struggled like a woman in

labor, blew themselves out.

The sea became calm,

the imhullu-wind grew quiet,

the flood held back.

I looked at the weather; silence reigned,

For all mankind had returned to clay....

I opened a porthole and light fell upon my cheeks....

Areas of land were emerging everywhere

The boat had come to rest on Mount Nimush."[11]

—Assyrian version of Epic Of Gilgamesh

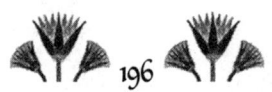

"Thinkest thou that I cannot now pray to my Father
and he shall presently give me more than
twelve legions of angels?"[12]

— Matthew 26:53

"And God saw that the wickedness of man was great in the

earth,

and that every imagination of the thoughts of his heart was

only evil continually.

And it repented the Lord that he had made man

on the earth,

and it grieved him at his heart.

And the Lord said,

I will destroy man whom I have created

from the face of the earth;

both man, and beast,

and the creeping thing,

and the fowls of the air;

for it repenteth me that I have made them.

But Noah found grace in the eyes of the Lord.

And God said unto Noah,

The end of all flesh is come before me;

for the earth is filled with violence through them; and, behold,

I will destroy them with the earth.

Make thee an ark of gopher wood;

rooms shalt thou make in the ark,

and shalt pitch it within and without with pitch.

And, behold, I, even I,

do bring a flood of waters upon the earth,

to destroy all flesh,

wherein is the breath of life,

from under heaven;

and every thing that is in the earth shall die.

But with thee will I establish my covenant;

and thou shalt come into the ark,

thou, and thy sons,

and thy wife, and thy sons wives with thee.

And of every living thing of all flesh,

two of every sort shalt thou bring into the ark,

to keep them alive with thee;

they shall be male and female.

Of fowls after their kind,

and of cattle after their kind,

of every creeping thing of the earth after his kind,

two of every sort shall come unto thee,

to keep them alive.

And take thou unto thee of all food that is eaten,

and thou shalt gather it to thee;

and it shall be for food for thee, and for them.

Thus did Noah;

according to all that God commanded him, so did he.

And the flood was forty days upon the earth;

and the waters increased,

and bare up the ark,

and it was lift up above the earth.

And every living substance was destroyed

which was upon the face of the ground, both man,

and cattle, and the creeping things,

and the fowl of the heaven;

and they were destroyed from the earth:

and Noah only remained alive,

and they that were with him in the ark.

And the waters prevailed upon the earth an

hundred and fifty days.

And the ark rested in the seventh month,

on the seventeenth day of the month,

upon the mountains of Ararat.

And the waters decreased continually until the tenth month:

in the tenth month,

on the first day of the month,

were the tops of the mountains seen.

And it came to pass at the end of forty days,

that Noah opened the window of the ark which he had

made:

And he sent forth a raven,

Which went forth to and fro,

until the waters were dried up from off the earth.

Also he sent forth a dove from him,

to see if the waters were abated from off the face of the

ground;

But the dove found no rest for the sole of her foot,

and she returned unto him into the ark,

for the waters were on the face of the whole earth:

then he put forth his hand,

and took her, and pulled her in unto him into the ark.

And he stayed yet other seven days;

and again he sent forth the dove out of the ark;

And the dove came in to him in the evening;

and, lo,

in her mouth was an olive leaf plucked off:

so Noah knew that the waters were abated from off the

earth.

And he stayed yet other seven days;

and sent forth the dove;

Which returned not again unto him any more.

And God spake unto Noah, saying,

Go forth of the ark,

thou, and thy wife, and thy sons,

and thy sons wives with thee.

Bring forth with thee every living thing that is with thee,

of all flesh,

both of fowl, and of cattle, and of every creeping thing

that creepeth upon the earth;

that they may breed abundantly in the earth,

and be fruitful,

and multiply upon the earth.

And Noah went forth,

and his sons, and his wife, and his sons wives with him:

Every beast,

every creeping thing, and every fowl,

and whatsoever creepeth upon the earth,

after their kinds,

went forth out of the ark."[13]

—Hebrew version of the *Story of the Flood* from
Genesis 6-8

"Gilgamesh spoke to Utanapishtim,

the Faraway:

I have been looking at you,

but your appearance is not strange –

you are like me!

You yourself are not different-

you are like me!

My mind was resolved to fight with you,

but instead? my arm lies useless over you.

Tell me,

how is it that you stand in the Assembly of the Gods,

and have found life!

Utanapishtim spoke to Gilgamesh, saying:

'I ill reveal to you, Gilgamesh,

a thing that is hidden,

a secret of the gods I will tell you!

Shuruppak, a city that you surely know,

situated on the banks of the Euphrates,

that city was very old,

and there were gods inside it.

The hearts of the Great Gods moved them to inflict the

Flood.

Their Father Anu uttered the oath of secrecy,

Valiant Enlil was their Adviser,

Ninurta was their Chamberlain,

Ennugi was their Minister of Canals.

Ea, the Clever Prince,

was under oath with them so he repeated their talk

to the reed house:

Reed house, reed house! Wall, wall!

Abandon wealth and seek living beings!

Spurn possessions and keep alive living beings!

Make all living beings go up into the boat.

The boat which you are to build,

its dimensions must measure equal to each other:

its length must correspond to its width.

Roof it over like the Apsu.

I understood and spoke to my lord, Ea:

My lord, thus is the command which you have uttered

I will heed and will do it.

But what shall I answer the city, the populace,

and the Elders! Ea spoke,

commanding me, his servant:

You, well then, this is what you must say to them:

It appears that Enlil is rejecting me

so I cannot reside in your city?

nor set foot on Enlil's earth.

I will go down to the Apsu to live with my lord, Ea,

and upon you he will rain down abundance,

a profusion of fowl, myriad! fishes.

He will bring to you a harvest of wealth,

in the morning he will let loaves of bread shower down,

and in the evening a rain of wheat!

Just as dawn began to glow

the land assembled around me,

the carpenter carried his hatchet,

the reed worker carried his flattening stone, the men,

The child carried the pitch,

the weak brought whatever else was needed.

On the fifth day I laid out her exterior.

It was a field in area,

its walls were each 10 times 12 cubits in height,

the sides of its top were of equal length, 10 times it cubits each.

I laid out its interior structure and drew a picture of it?.

I provided it with six decks,

thus dividing it into seven levels.

The inside of it I divided into nine compartments.

I drove plugs to keep out water in its middle part.

I saw to the punting poles and laid in what was necessary.

Three times 3,600 units of raw bitumen

I poured into the bitumen kiln,

three times 3,600 units of pitch into it,

there were three times 3,600 porters of casks

who carried vegetable oil,

apart from the 3,600 units of oil which they consumed!

and two times 3,600 units of oil which the boatman stored

away.

I butchered oxen for the meat!,

and day upon day I slaughtered sheep.

I gave the workmen? ale, beer, oil, and wine,

as if it were river water,

so they could make a party like the New Year's

Festival.

and I set my hand to the oiling!.

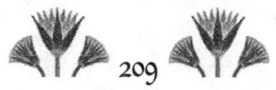

The boat was finished by sunset.

The launching was very difficult.

They had to keep carrying a runway of poles front to

back,

until two-thirds of it had gone

into the water?.

Whatever I had I loaded on it:

whatever silver I had I loaded on it,

whatever gold I had I loaded on it.

All the living beings that I had I loaded on it,

I had all my kith and kin go up into the boat,

all the beasts and animals of the field and the craftsmen I

had go up.

Shamash had set a stated time:

In the morning I will let loaves of bread shower down,

and in the evening a rain of wheat!

Go inside the boat, seal the entry!

That stated time had arrived.

In the morning he let loaves of bread shower down,

and in the evening a rain of wheat.

I watched the appearance of the weather,

the weather was frightful to behold!

I went into the boat and sealed the entry.

For the caulking of the boat,

to Puzuramurri, the boatman,

I gave the palace together with its contents.

Just as dawn began to glow there arose from the horizon a

black cloud.

Adad rumbled inside of it,

before him went Shullat and Hanish,

heralds going over mountain and land.

Erragal pulled out the mooring poles,

forth went Ninurta and made the dikes overflow.

The Anunnaki lifted up the torches,

setting the land ablaze with their flare.

Stunned shock over Adad's deeds overtook the heavens,

and turned to blackness all that had been light.

The land shattered like a pot.

All day long the South Wind blew,

blowing fast,

submerging the mountain in water,

overwhelming the people like an attack.

No one could see his fellow,

they could not recognize each other in the torrent.

The gods were frightened by the Flood,

and retreated,

ascending to the heaven of Anu.

The gods were cowering like dogs,

crouching by the outer wall.

Ishtar shrieked like a woman in childbirth,

the sweet-voiced Mistress of the Gods wailed:

The olden days have alas turned to clay,

because I said evil things in the Assembly of the Gods!

How could I say evil things in the

Assembly of the Gods,

ordering a catastrophe to destroy my people!!

No sooner have I given birth to my dear people

than they fill the sea like so many fish!

The gods-those of the Anunnaki-were weeping with her,

the gods humbly sat weeping, sobbing with grief?

their lips burning, parched with thirst.

Six days and seven nights came the wind and flood,

the storm flattening the land.

When the seventh day arrived,

the storm was pounding,

the flood was a war...

struggling with itself like a woman writhing in labor.

The sea calmed, fell still,

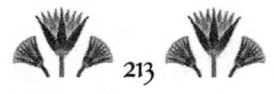

the whirlwind and flood stopped up.

I looked around all day long—

quiet had set in and all the human beings had turned to clay!

The terrain was as flat as a roof.

I opened a vent and fresh air daylight!

fell upon the side of my nose.

I fell to my knees and sat weeping,

tears streaming down the side of my nose.

I looked around for coastlines in the expanse of the sea,

and at twelve leagues there emerged a region of land.

On Mt. Nimush the boat lodged firm,

Mt. Nimush held the boat,

Allowing no sway.

One day and a second,

Mt. Nimush held the boat,

Allowing no sway.

A third day, a fourth,

Mt. Nimush held the boat,

Allowing no sway.

A fifth day, a sixth,

Mt. Nimush held the boat,

Allowing no sway.

When a seventh day arrived

I sent forth a dove and released it.

The dove went off, but came back to me;

no perch was visible so it circled back to me.

I sent forth a swallow and released it.

The swallow went off, but came back to me;

no perch was visible so it circled back to me.

I sent forth a raven and released it.

The raven went off,

and saw the waters slither back.

It eats, it scratches, it bobs, but does not circle back to me.

Then I sent out everything in all directions

215

and sacrificed a sheep.

I offered incense in front of the mountain-ziggurat.

Seven and seven cult vessels I put in place,

and into the fire underneath or

into their bowls I poured

reeds, cedar, and myrtle.

The gods smelled the savor,

the gods smelled the sweet savor,

and collected like flies over a sheep sacrifice.

Just then Beletili arrived.

She lifted up the large flies beads

which Anu had made for his enjoyment!:

You gods, as surely as I shall not forget this lapis lazuli

around my neck,

may I be mindful of these days, and never forget them!

The gods may come to the incense offering,

but Enlil may not come to the incense offering,

because without considering he brought about the Flood

and consigned my people to annihilation.

Just then Enlil arrived.

He saw the boat and became furious,

he was filled with rage at the Igigi gods:

Where did a living being escape?

No man was to survive the annihilation!

Ninurta spoke to Valiant Enlil, saying:

Who else but Ea could devise such a thing?

It is Ea who knows every machination!

Ea spoke to Valiant Enlil, saying:

It is yours, O Valiant One,

who is the Sage of the Gods.

How, how could you bring about a Flood

without consideration charge the violation to the violator,

charge the offense to the offender,

but be compassionate lest mankind be cut off,

be patient lest they be killed.

Instead of your bringing on the Flood,

Would that a lion had appeared to diminish the people!

Instead of your bringing on the Flood,

Would that a Wolf had appeared to diminish the people!

Instead of your bringing on the Flood,

Would that famine had occurred to slay the land!

Instead of your bringing on the Flood,

Would that Pestilent Erra had appeared to ravage the

land!

It was not I who revealed the secret of the Great Gods,

I only made a dream appear to Atrahasis,

and thus he heard the secret of the gods.

Now then!

The deliberation should be about him!

Enlil went up inside the boat and, grasping my hand,

made me go up.

He had my wife go up and kneel by my side.
He touched our forehead and, standing between us,
he blessed us:
Previously Utanapishtim was a human being.
But now let Utanapishtim and his wife become like us,
the gods!
Let Utanapishtim reside far away,
at the Mouth of the Rivers.
They took us far away and settled us at the Mouth of
the Rivers.
Now then, who will convene the gods on your behalf,
that you may find the life that you are seeking!
Wait!
You must not lie down for six days and seven nights.
soon as he sat down with his head between his legs
sleep, like a fog, blew upon him.
Utanapishtim said to his wife:

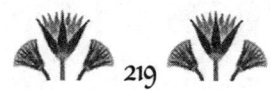

Look there! The man, the youth who wanted eternal
life!

Sleep, like a fog, blew over him.

His wife said to Utanapishtim the Faraway:

Touch him, let the man awaken.

Let him return safely by the way he came.

Let him return to his land by the gate through which he
left.

Utanapishtim said to his wife:

Mankind is deceptive, and will deceive you.

Come, bake leaves for him and keep setting them by his head

and draw on the wall each day that he lay down.

She baked his leaves and placed them by his head

and marked on the wall the day that he lay down.

The first loaf was dessicated,

the second stale, the third moist?,

the fourth turned white, its ,

the fifth sprouted gray mold,

the sixth is still fresh.

The seventh, suddenly he touched him and the man awoke.

Gilgamesh said to Utanapishtim:

The very moment sleep was pouring over me

you touched me and alerted me!

Utanapishtim spoke to Gilgamesh, saying:

Look over here, Gilgamesh, count your loaves!

You should be aware of what is marked on the wall!

Your first loaf is dessicated,

the second stale, the third moist,

your fourth turned white,

its the fifth sprouted gray mold,

the sixth is still fresh.

The seventh, suddenly he touched him and the man awoke.

Gilgamesh said to Utanapishtim the Faraway:

O woe! What shall I do, Utanapishtim,

Where shall I go!

The Snatcher has taken hold of my flesh,

in my bedroom Death dwells,

and wherever I set foot there too is Death!

Home Empty-Handed.

Utanapishtim said to Urshanabi, the ferryman:

May the harbor reject you,

may the ferry landing reject you

May you who used to walk its shores be denied its shores!

The man in front of whom you walk,

matted hair chains his body,

animal skins have ruined his beautiful skin.

Take him away, Urshanabi,

bring him to the washing place.

Let him wash his matted hair in water like ellu.

Let him cast away his animal skin and have the sea

carry it off,

let his body be moistened with fine oil,

let the wrap around his head be made new,

let him wear royal robes worthy of him!

Until he goes off to his city,

until he sets off on his way,

let his royal robe not become spotted,

let it be perfectly new!

Urshanabi took him away and brought him to

the washing place.

He washed his matted hair with water like ellu.

He cast off his animal skin and the sea carried it off.

He moistened his body with fine oil,

and made a new wrap for his head.

He put on a royal robe worthy of him.

Until he went away to his city,

until he set off on his way,

his royal robe remained unspotted,

223

it was perfectly clean.

Gilgamesh and Urshanabi boarded the boat,

they cast off the magillu-boat, and sailed away.

The wife of Utanapishtim the Faraway said to him:

Gilgamesh came here exhausted and worn out.

What can you give him so that he can return

to his land with honor!

Then Gilgamesh raised a punting pole and drew the boat

to shore.

Utanapishtim spoke to Gilgamesh,

saying: Gilgamesh,

you came here exhausted and worn out.

What can I give you so you can return to your land?

I will disclose to you a thing that is hidden, Gilgamesh,

I will tell you.

There is a plant like a boxthorn,

whose thorns will prick your hand like a rose.

If your hands reach that plant you will become a

young man again.

Hearing this, Gilgamesh opened a conduit

to the Apsu and attached heavy stones to his feet.

They dragged him down,

to the Apsu they pulled him.

He took the plant, though it pricked his hand,

and cut the heavy stones from his feet,

letting the waves throw him onto its shores.

Gilgamesh spoke to Urshanabi, the ferryman, saying:

Urshanabi, this plant is a plant against decay!

by which a man can attain his survival!.

I will bring it to Uruk-Haven,

and have an old man eat the plant to test it.

The plant's name is The Old Man Becomes a

Young Man.

Then I will eat it and return to the condition of my
youth.

At twenty leagues they broke for some food,

at thirty leagues they stopped for the night.

Seeing a spring and how cool its waters were,

Gilgamesh went down and was bathing in the water.

A snake smelled the fragrance of the plant,

silently came up and carried off the plant.

While going back it sloughed off its casing.

At that point Gilgamesh sat down, weeping,

his tears streaming over the side of his nose.

Counsel me, O ferryman Urshanabi!

For whom have my arms labored, Urshanabi!

For whom has my heart's blood roiled!

I have not secured any good deed for myself,

but done a good deed for the lion of the ground!

Now the high waters are coursing twenty leagues distant,

as I was opening the conduit?

I turned my equipment over into it!.

What can I find to serve as a marker? for me!

I will turn back from the journey by sea and leave the boat

by the shore!

At twenty leagues they broke for some food,

at thirty leagues they stopped for the night.

They arrived in Uruk-Haven.

Gilgamesh said to Urshanabi, the ferryman:

Go up, Urshanabi, onto the wall of Uruk

and walk around.

Examine its foundation,

inspect its brickwork thoroughly,

is not even the core of the brick structure of kiln-fired brick,

and did not the Seven Sages themselves

lay out its plan!

One league city, one league palm gardens,

one league lowlands,

the open area of the Ishtar Temple,

three leagues and the open area of Uruk it encloses."[14]

—Sumerian version of The Epic of Gilgamesh

The Source of Being

"Theosophy endeavors to present to man what his real
nature is; that he is first, last, and all the time Spirit.
Spirit means Life and Consciousness –
the power to see, to know, to experience.
We all have that.
That is common to all of us.
It is not separate in itself –
it is the One Life in all beings of every grade.
But we, as individuals, have evolved into individuals from
the great Ocean of Life.
We are Individualized Spirit,
and so we each have a separate individual existence,
which is continuous.
In that sense we are an evolution,
but an evolution of Spirit, not Matter –

an evolution of Knowledge, not of form only.

This has been obtained through observation and experience;

Whatever differences exist are because of more or less

experience,

or a better adaptation and application of it;

there is no difference in the Source or Potentialities

of any being."[15]

—Robert Crosbie

Theosophy Magazine

"Every living creature and thing on earth,

including man,

evolved from *one common primal form.*

Physical man must have passed

through the same stages of the evolutionary process in the

various modes of procreation as other animals have:

he must have divided himself;

then, hermaphrodite,

have given birth *parthenogenetically*

on the 'immaculate principle' to his young ones;

the next stage would be the *oviparous* –

at first without any fructifying element,

then with the help of the fertilitary spore;

and only after the final and definite evolution of both sexes,

would he become a distinct male and female,

when reproduction through sexual union would grow into

universal law.

So far,

all this is scientifically proven.

There was a 'special creation' for man,

and a 'special creation' for the ape,

his progeny;

only on other lines than ever bargained for by Science...

man was indeed made in the image of a type projected by his

progenitor,

the creating Angel-Force,

or Dhyan Chohan;

while the wanderer of the forest of Sumatra

was made *in the image of man,*

since the framework of the ape,

we say again,

is the revival,

the resuscitation by abnormal means of the actual form

232

of the Third-Round and of the Fourth-Round
Man as well, later on.

Nothing is lost in nature,

not an atom....

Owing to the very type of his development man *cannot*

descend from either an ape or an ancestor common to both,

but shows his origin from a type far superior to himself.

And this type is the Heavenly man –

the Dyhan Chohans,

or the Pitris so-called.

On the other hand, the pithecoids,

the orang-outang,

the gorilla,

and the chimpanzee *can*, and,

as the Occult Sciences teach, do,

descend from the animalized Fourth human Root-Race,

being the product of man and an extinct species of mammal –

Whose *remote* ancestors were themselves the product of
Lemurian bestiality –
Which lived in the Miocene age,
originating in the sin of the 'Mind-less' races of the middle
Third Race period.
All forms which now people the earth,
are so many variations on *basic types* originally thrown off
by the 'Man'
of the Third and Fourth Round."[16]

—Helena P. Blavatsky
The Races of Man: The Missing Link

234

"Nature always,

so to speak,

knows where and when to stop.

Greater even than the mystery of natural growth is the

mystery of the natural cessation of growth.

There is a measure in all natural things –

in their size,

speed or violence.

As a result, the system of nature,

of which man is a part,

tends to be self-balancing, self-adjusting, self-cleansing."[17]

—E. F. Schumacher
Enlightenment Magazine

"The Adam was formed in Creation year 0,

or the year 3996 BC.

Seth was born when The Adam was 130 years old,

130 years after Creation,

or the year 3866 BC.

Enos was born when Seth was 105 years old,

235 years after Creation,

or the year 3761 BC.

Cainan was born when Enos was 90 years old,

325 years after Creation,

or the year 3671 BC.

Mehalaleel was born when Cainan was 70 years old,

395 years after Creation,

or the year 3601 BC.

Jared was born when Mehalaleel was 65 years old,

460 years after Creation,

or the year 3536 BC.

Enoch was born when Jared was 162 years old,

622 years after Creation,

or the year 3374 BC.

Methuselah was born when Enoch was 65 years old,

687 years after Creation,

or the year 3309 BC.

Lamech was born when Methuselah was 187 years old,

874 years after Creation,

or the year 3122 BC.

Noah was born when Lamech was 182 years old,

1056 years after Creation,

or the years 2940 BC.

Flood year was when Noah was 600 years old,

1,656 years after Creation, or the year 2340 BC."[18]

— Antediluvian Patriarchs and the Date of The
Flood from Genesis

237

"*Bereshith bara elohim et hashamayim et ha-aretz,*

the first sentence of Genesis in Hebrew.

The theosophists point out that it has two meanings.

If the division is made thusly,

beresh yithbara, be-resh

i.e., head, wisdom, knowledge, higher part, first in a series,

Head or knowledge made Itself Into Heaven and

Earth,

out of previously present material?.

That is, The gods,

through wisdom,

carved *yithbara,*

the heaven and the material sphere."[19]

—*Bereshith ~Genesis 1.1~, The Torah*

238

"From the Sephiroth descend the four root races,

each issuing from the one above it,

the lower swallowing the higher:

atziluth -- the first and most spiritual race;

briah -- the second race composed of the servants of the first;

yetzirah, the third race mankind being a fallen sub-race

thereof comprised of

cherubim, seraphim, lucifer, elohim and the sons of god.

Finally, there is the fourth race;

assiah, containing the atlanteans and the qliphoth.

Incidentally, man, having sinned,

is imprisoned in the material world with its eternal

reincarnations as punishment until he manages to purify

himself."[20]

—E. E. Rehmus

The Magician's Dictionary

"Enoch was the son of Cain,
father of Methuselah.
Enochian was the pre-Babel language.
Enochian was the angelic language used in his calls and
aethyrs."[21]

—E. E. Rehmus
The Magician's Dictionary

"Elohim, Hebrew, plural of God,

usually translated as the divine plural,

indicating the singular, but the word is clearly,

undeniably plural.

As most of the book of Genesis comes from Egypt,

Babylon and Persia,

the word probably derives from Egyptian ali,

Babylonian ili, or the 7 gods of the original cosmos.

The names of the original seven Hebrew,

pre-Judaic *elohim* were probably,

ialdabaoth, jehovah, sabaoth,

adonai, oreus, eloeus and *astanphaeus.*

The last three have obviously been altered through

gnosticism, which explains their anomalous Graeco-Latin

endings."[22]

—Eliphas Levi, The Nuctameron of the Hebrews

241

"Beings who lived in water,
half-humanoid and half-fish,
have been credited with the founding and origins of many
civilizations on earth.
Water-beings have been described as responsible for
teaching and assisting humanity in areas such as agriculture,
arts, cosmology,
laws, mathematics,
temple-building and music."[23]

—Robert Temple
The Sirius Mystery

"Angels are purely mental entities
acting as messengers between biodes ∽flesh-entities∽
and theodes ∽spirit-entities∽."[24]

—E. E. Rehmus
The Magician's Dictionary

"I have encountered a few creationists

and because they were usually nice,

intelligent people,

I have been unable to decide whether they were really mad,

or only pretending to be mad.

If I was a religious person,

I would consider creationism nothing less than blasphemy.

Do its adherents imagine that God is a cosmic hoaxer

who has created that whole vast fossil record for the sole

purpose of misleading mankind?

And, although I do not necessarily agree with

paleontologist Teilhard de Chardin's advocacy of

evolution as a proof of the glory of God,

de Chardin's attitude is both logical and inspiring.

A creator who laid the foundations for the entire future

at the beginning of time

is far more awesome

than a clumsy tinkerer who constantly modifies his creations

and throws away

entire species in the process.

Even the Vatical,[i]

while firm in its declaration that the human soul is divinely

created and not subject to process,

has stated that the theory of physical evolution is more than

just a hypothesis." [25]

—Sir Arthur Charles Clark
On Creationism, In Science

---

[i] "Vatical: resembling or characteristic of a prophet or prophecy; 'the high priest's divinatory pronouncement'; 'mantic powers'; 'a kind of sibylline book with ready and infallible answers to questions'"-*The American Heritage® Dictionary of the English Language.*

"If I were going to construct a God,
I would furnish Him with some ways and qualities
and characteristics which the Present Bible one lacks...
He would spend some of His eternities in trying to
forgive Himself
for making man unhappy
when He could have made him happy
with the same effort
and He would spend the rest of them in studying
astronomy."[26]

— Mark Twain's Notebook 1896

Chapter 4

The Claiming of Humanity

Fig. 6. A Medieval Hebrew Bible manuscript scroll, known as *The Masoretic Text*. In terms of the masoretic text the word *mesorah* has a very specific meaning: it refers to concise marginal notes in manuscripts (and later printings) of the Hebrew Bible which note textual details, usually about the precise spelling of words.

"My religion consists of a humble admiration of the
illimitable superior spirit
who reveals himself in the slight details
we are able to perceive with our frail and feeble minds."[1]

—Albert Einstein

"All are architects of Fate,
Working in these walls of Time;
Some with massive deeds and great,
Some with ornaments of rhyme.

Nothing useless is, or low;
Each thing in its place is best;
And what seems but idle show
Strengthens and supports the rest.

For the structure that we raise,
Time is with materials filled;
Our to-days and yesterdays
Are the blocks with which we build.

Truly shape and fashion these;
Leave no yawning gaps between;

Think not, because no man sees,
Such things will remain unseen.

In the elder days of Art,
Builders wrought with greatest care
Each minute and unseen part;
For the Gods see everywhere.

Let us do our work as well,
Both the unseen and the seen;
Make the house, where Gods may dwell,
Beautiful, entire, and clean.

Else our lives are incomplete,
Standing in these walls of Time,
Broken stairways, where the feet
Stumble as they seek to climb.

Build to-day, then, strong and sure,
With a firm and ample base;
And ascending and secure
Shall to-morrow find its place.

Thus alone can we attain
To those turrets, where the eye
Sees the world as one vast plain,
And one boundless reach of sky."[2]

—Henry Wadsworth Longfellow
The Builders

"The Science of Will,

the principal of all wisdom and the source of all power,

is contained in twenty-two Arcana or symbolic hieroglyphs,

each of whose attributes conceals a certain meaning and which,

taken as a whole,

compose an absolute doctrine memorized by its correspondence

with the Letters of the sacred language and with the

Numbers that are connected with these Letters.

Each Letter and each Number,

contemplated by the eye or uttered by the mouth,

expresses a reality of the divine world, the *intellectual world*,

and the *physical world*."[3]

—Antoine Court de Gebelin

"The value of life is not measured by the weight of its
accumulated baubles of glass....
Knowledge is an accumulation of vision.

If I have seen farther,
it is by standing on the shoulders of giants."[4]

—Sir Isaac Newton

"It always strikes me,

and it is very peculiar,

that whenever we see the image of indescribable

and unutterable desolation –

of loneliness,

poverty,

and misery,

the end and extreme of things,

the thought of God comes to one's mind."[5]

—Vincent Van Gogh

"Inhumanity has a great future."[6]

—Paul Valery
Collected Works

"There is nothing commonplace in the world except the mental attitude of man."[7]

—Charles Burchfield

"There is no one, there are no people.

It is desolate; it lies desolate,

misery emerges,

misery spreads...."[8]

— Technicians of the Sacred
Ancient Aztec Song

"Man, saith Solomon,

that can hardly discern the things that are upon the earth,

and with great labor find out the things that are before us;

that hath so short a time in the world,

as he no sooner begins to learn,

than to die;

that borrowed knowledge in his understanding nothing truly;

that is ignorant of the essence of his own soul,

and which the wisest of the naturalists,

if Aristotle be he, could never so much as define

but the action and effect, but that God created it!"[9]

—Honoré de Balzac
The Magic Skin

"Once to every man and nation comes the moment to decide.

In the strife of Truth with Falsehood,

for the good or evil side.

Some great cause, God's new Messiah,

offering each the bloom or blight.

Part the goats up the left hand,

and the sheep upon the right.

And the choice goes by forever twixt that darkness and that

light."[10]

—James Russell Lowell
The Present Crisis

"The future is not in danger of revelations of Science.

Science is truth;

Truth loves the truth.

Changes must come and old things

must pass away,

but no tree sheds its leaf until it has rolled up a bud

at its axil for the next summer."[11]

–H. W. Beecher
Progress of Thought in the Church

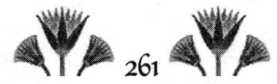

261

"What I must do is all that concerns me,

not what people think....

It is easy in the world to live after the world's opinion;

it is easy in solitude to live after our own;

but the great man is he who in the midst of the crowd keeps

with

perfect sweetness the independence of solitude."[12]

—Ralph Waldo Emerson
Self-Reliance

"Every man, in every condition,

is great.

It is only our own diseased sight which makes him little....

His powers of intellect,

of conscience, of love, of knowing God,

of perceiving the beautiful,

of acting on his own mind,

on outward nature,

and on his fellow creatures,

these are glorious prerogatives."[13]

—William Ellery Channing
Address on Self-Culture

"Out of the flesh,

out of the minds and hearts

Of thousand upon thousand common men,

Cranks,

martyrs,

starry-eyed enthusiasts,

Slow-spoken neighbors,

hard to push around,

Women whose hands were gentle with their kids

And men with a cold passion for mere justice.

We made this thing,

this dream." [14]

—Stephen Vincent Benet
The Making of a Dream

"We ought to esteem it of the greatest importance that the fictions which children first hear should be adapted in the most perfect manner to the promotion of virtue."[15]

—Plato

"Then Almitra spoke, saying,

We would ask now of death.

And he said:

You would know the secret of death.

But how shall you find it unless you seek it in the heath of

life?

The owl whose night-bound eyes are blind unto the day

cannot unveil the mystery of light.

If you would indeed behold the spirit of death,

open your heart wide unto the body of life.

For life and death are one,

even as the river and sea are one.

In the depth of your hopes and desires lies your silent

knowledge of the beyond;

and like seeds dreaming beneath the snow your heart dreams

of spring.

Trust the dreams,

for in them is hidden the gate to eternity.

Your fear of death is but the trembling of the shepherd

when he stands before the king whose hand is to be laid upon

him in honor.

Is the shepherd not joyful beneath his trembling,

that he shall wear the mark of the king?

Yet is he not more mindful of his trembling?

For what is it to die but to stand naked in the wind and to

melt into the sun? And what is it to cease breathing,

but to free the breath from its restless tides,

that it may rise and expand and seek God unencumbered?

Only when you drink from the river of silence shall you

indeed sing. And when you have reached the mountain top,

then you shall begin to climb. And when the earth shall

claim your limbs, then shall you truly dance."[16]

—Khalil Gibran, The Prophet

267

"I believe that humanity shall accept as an axiom

for its conduct the principle

for which I have laid down my life –

the right to investigate.

It is the credo of free men –

this opportunity to try, this privilege to err,

this courage to experiment anew."[17]

–Roger Bacon

"Reading maketh a full man,

conference a ready man,

and writing and exact man;

and, therefore,

if a man write little,

he had need have a great memory;

if he confer little,

he had need have a present wit;

and if he read little,

he had need have much cunning,

to seem to know that he doth not."[18]

—Lord Francis Bacon
Essay on Studies

"Be less inquisitive about people,
and more inquisitive about ideas."[19]

—Madame Marie Curie

"The music I have written is nothing compared to the music I have heard."[20]

—Ludwig Von Beethoven

"They have but few laws, and such is their constitution
that they need not many.
They do very much condemn other nations, whose laws,
together with the comments on them,
swell up so many volumes;
for they think it an unreasonable thing
to oblige men to obey a body of laws
that cannot be read or understood by every one of the subjects.
They have no lawyers among them,
for they consider them as a sort of people whose profession it is
to disguise matters as well as to wrest laws."[21]

—Sir Thomas More
Utopia, of their laws

"He that will write well in any tongue must follow this
counsel of Aristotle,
to speak as the common people do,
and think as wise men do."[22]

—Roger Ascham
The Schoolmaster

"Doth any man doubt that if there were taken out of men's

minds various opinions,

flattering hopes,

false valuations,

imaginations as one would,

and the like,

it would leave the minds

of a number of men poor shrunken things,

full of melancholy and indisposition,

and unpleasing to themselves?"[23]

—Lord Bacon
Essay on Truth

"Bee humble to thy superiors; gentle to thy equals;

to thy inferiors favourable.

Envie not thy betters, justle not thy fellows;

oppress not the poore.

The stipend that is allowed to maintain thee use wisely,

be neither prodigall to spende all,

covetous to keep all.

Cut they coat according to thy cloth,

and thinke it better to bee accompted thriftie among the wise

than a good companion among the riotous."[24]

—John Lyly
Euphues: Anatomy of Wit

"Give me the liberty to know,

to utter,

and to argue freely,

above all liberties." [25]

–John Milton

Areopagitica

"He who knows wrath,

knows pride;

he who knows pride, knows deceit; he who knows deceit,

knows greed;

he who knows greed, knows love; he who knows love,

knows hate;

he who knows hate, knows delusion; he who knows delusion,

knows conception;

he who knows conception, knows birth; he who knows birth,

knows death;

he who knows death, knows hell; he who knows hell,

knows animal existence;

he who knows animal existence,

knows pain.

Therefore, a wise man should avoid wrath, pride, deceit,

greed, love, hate, delusion, conception, birth, death, hell,

animal existence, and pain.

This is the doctrine of the Seer,

Who does not injure living beings and has put an end

to acts and to samsara.

Preventing the propensity to sin destroys former actions.

Is there any worldly weakness in the Seer?

There exists none, there is none.

Thus I say." [26]

—Jaina Sutras
Prakrit and Sacred Books of the East

278

"...to know oneself, at the deepest level,

is simultaneously

to know god:

this is the secret of gnosis....

Self-knowledge is knowledge of god;

the self and the divine are identical."[27]

— Elaine Pagels, Eminent scholar of Gnosticism

"We are autochthonous peoples,

that is,

we are an integral part of the very lands and waters

we have traditionally used and occupied.

Our identify and culture is firmly rooted in these

lands and waters.

It is this relationship which constitutes the very unique

features of our cultural identity

in contrast to the cultures of other peoples within each of the

countries from which we come."[28]

—Ellen Boye
Grönland

"From the earth the Creating Power formed the shapes

of men and women.

He used red earth and white earth,

black earth and yellow earth,

and made as many as he thought would do for a start.

He stamped out on the earth and the shapes came alive,

each taking the color of the earth

out of which it was made.

The Creating Power gave all of them understanding

and speech

and told them what tribes they belonged to."[29]

—Leonard Crow Dog
American Myths and Legends

281

"The land, of course,
must be transferred from the hands of the Natives
to those of the Whites....
So the Natives must give way and either become servants
of the Whites
or withdraw to the reserves allotted to them."[30]

–John H. Wellington
Newspaper Article, German Southwest Africa, 1901

"If reform is necessary,

it ought to be carried out after preparation and with due

consideration,

leaving the subject people under the illusion that their old

traditions will be maintained,

even if they are in fact being gradually unobtrusively,

progressively, modified—as is necessary.

That seems to be sound psychology."[31]

—René Maunier
The Sociology of the Colonies

"You are a child of the universe,
no less than the trees and the stars;
you have a right to be here." [32]

—Max Ehrmann
Desiderata

"Patanjali,
in the *Yoga Sutra*,
tells us that war can be stopped
only by a superior understanding of the human condition."[33]

—David Appelbaum
Can War Be Stopped

"It is those who cannot see straight who fall into error:

This is the sightedness of the man who denies God's attributes.

Ah, the pity!

Nobody possesses the power:
Eyes blind and the world filled with sunlight!"[34]

—Fariduddin 'Attar, 12th century

"It is not strange, then,

that there exists the cruel procedure known as *correlias*,

which consists of surprising the habitations of some tribe

and taking the members of it prisoner.

These prisoners are taken to far territories and are

dedicated to work....

This catechization has the advantage that the individual

soon obtains precise concepts of the importance that his

personal work has in the commerce of civilized people....

In our century,

the procedure is cruel and wounds all the fibers of our

sensibility;

but one must recognize the powerful and rapid help that it

lends to civilization." [35]

—S. Palacios i. Mendiburu
Boletin de la Sociedad Geografica de Lima

"Much of the nation will wish for negotiation
between great Lords who are responsible for the war,
but no one will listen to anything.

Alas!
If only God would send peace to the Earth!"[36]

—Michel de Nostradamus
Nostradamus & The Millennium

"We tried to exterminate a native race,

whom our lack of wisdom had goaded into rebellion."[37]

—German Professor Boon,
in lecture to the Royal Colonial Institute of London

"The origin of all wars is the pursuit of wealth,
and we are forced to pursue wealth because we live
in slavery to the care of the body."[38]

—Plato
Phaedo

"Contact with European culture has given them a

knowledge of great wealth,

opportunity and privilege,

but only very limited avenues by which

to acquire these things."[39]

—Ron Crocombe

New Guinea

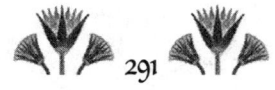

"If, actuated by egotism, thou thinkest:

'I will not fight,'

in vain is this thy resolve.

Thine own nature will impel thee."[40]

—Bhagavad-Gita, xviii 59

"Up, Up,
Only a little life is left,
the road before you is long,
and you are immersed in illusion."[41]

—Persian saying

"The land is of the Indian.

The Indian is the earth itself.

The Indian is the owner of the land,

with property titles or without them."[42]

—Miguel Chase-Sardi
Por la Liberación del Indigena

"Easter Island,

the marooned home of mankind's Third Race,

which, after having stripped the island of trees,

vegetation and animals,

resorted to cannibalism and mass murder, suicide."[43]

—E. E. Rehmus
The Magician's Dictionary

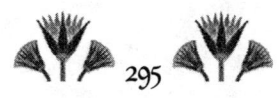

"Our plea to the world is to help us in our struggle
to find a place in the world community where we can exercise
our right to self-determination as a distinct people and as a
nation."[44]

—Mel Watkins
The Dene Declaration

"Without unity we will never have the force to defend our land and the future of our children."[45]

—Unidad Indigena, 1975
regarding Indian Unity in Columbia

"Man perfected by society is the best of all animals;
he is the most terrible of all when he lives without law,
and without justice."[46]

—Aristotle

"To be satisfied with a little,

is the greatest wisdom;

and he that increaseth his riches,

increaseth his cares;

but a contented mind is a hidden treasure,

and trouble findeth it not." [47]

—Akhenaten

"The world is my country,
all mankind are my brethren,
and to do good is my religion."[48]

—Thomas Paine

Chapter 5

Tales of Ancient Egypt, Thoth-Hermes & Mercury

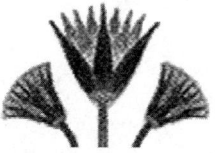

Fig. 7. Map of the Earliest Civilizations.

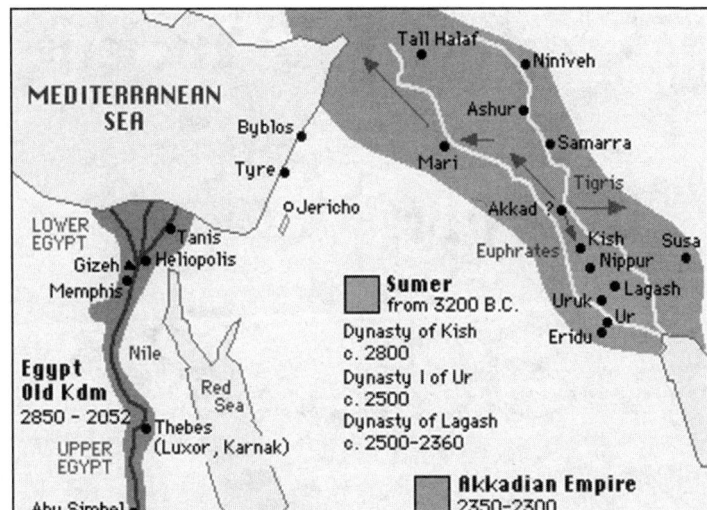

"...the river gave its name to the country,

for Aegyptus

was originally the name of the river

now known both in Egypt and elsewhere in the world

as the Nile...

there is sufficient evidence in Homer,

where we find the statement that Menelaus brought up

'at the mouth of the Aegyptus.'"[1]

—Aubrey De Sélincourt
Arrian: The Campaigns of Alexander

"The Book of the Dead,

though it appears to be a ritual for funerary rites

of a deceased king or high official,

was actually a description of the trials,

temptations and difficulties which the adept had to meet

and overcome as he progressed

from knowledge to knowledge

and from power to power,

as he penetrated the superphysical regions from plane to

plane.

The ultimate goal of initiation,

was 'full realization of the essential divine nature of man,

the recovery by the individual of

the full knowledge and powers of his divine spiritual nature,

of that which he is now dead through

the 'Fall of Man' into matter and physical life.'

There had been three important Egyptian practices

---

[i] Thoth, the Atlantean, is said to be the author the *Book of the Dead*.

304

performed in the Holy of Holies
of the Great Pyramid:
the convocation of disembodied entities,
either of 'gods' or of spirits of the dead;
divination through a child medium;
and, finally,
some form of spiritual and physical regeneration....
The esoteric doctrines practiced in the temples along the
Valley of Nile was 'an intimacy with the ancient 'gods'
of Egypt and of enticing their participation
into the life of Man.'"[2]

—William Kingsland
The Great Pyramid in Fact and in Theory

305

"The Crata Repoa is a reconstruction
of the rituals of initiation into the ancient mysteries
put together from hints and allusions
contained in the writings of such classical authors as
Porphyry, Herodotus,
Iamblichus, Apuleius,
Tertullian, Heliodorus,
Lucian Rufinus, and others.
From these fragments insight can be gained into the degrees
of initiation undergone between neophyte and adept...
the third degree of the Crata Repoa
corresponds closely to the third degree of the Blue Lodge
of Modern Freemasonry."[3]

—Manly P. Hall
Freemasonry and the Ancient Egyptians

306

"According to Sumerian legend,

it was at his temple at Eridu,

present day Kuwait,

Iraq region,

that Ea,

the Lord of Earth,

and the guardian of the secrets of all scientific knowledge,

stored the 'me' Tablets of Destiny.

These crystal-like objects,

sometimes worn as ornaments on the body of the gods,

contained divine knowledge including astronomy,

astrology and temple-building.

In myth, the 'me' pronounced 'may'

also contained the healing secrets of the gods.

In ancient Egypt,

'me' denotes rebirth of the dead.

Today 'me' is the root for such words as Medicine,

meditation, and meme songs,

stories, ideas, beliefs."[4]

—William Henry
Language of the Birds

"He waited for the hour of the day
when the length of his shadow
was exactly equal
to the height of his person,
and then measured the length of the pyramid's shadow.

'This, gentlemen,' he said,
'is the exact height of the Great Pyramid.'"[5]

—Archimedes

"Doctor of the Planispheres, Hermetic Philosopher,
Grand Elect of the Eons,
Knight Prince of the Rose of Heredom,
Grand Master of the Temple of Wisdom,
Knight Noachite,
Wise Siviast,
Knight Supreme Commander of the Stars,
Sublime, Sage of the Zodiac,
Shepherd Kind of the Hutz,
Interpreter of Hieroglyphs, Sage of the Pyramids,
Sublime Titan of the Caucasus,
Orphic Doctor, Sublime Skald,
Prince Brahmin, Guardian of the Three Fires."[6]

—Grades of the Ancient and Primitive
Memphis-Misraim Rite of Freemasonry

"The angels or divine messengers,

servants of eternal Providence,

are spirits more perfect in essence than men.

They help us, yet without restricting our will,

which is always free to choose between good and evil.

They work out the plan of the various ordeals to which

every human being is submitted during earthly life;

they give an account of our actions to

God and lead our souls after death

into the region of rewards and expiations."[7]

—Iamblichus
Treatise on the Egyptian Mysteries

311

"Osiris...
Lord of Creation;
Son of Man; King of Egypt."[8]

–Sir E. A. Wallis Budge
The Book of the Dead

"The highest wisdom of the ancients believed in the mysterious connection of the name and the being who holds it as if it were a divine or infernal talisman that could either illuminate his passage through life or destroy it in flames.

The Magi of Egypt confided this secret to Pythagoras, who transmitted it to the Greeks.

In the sacred alphabet of Magism,

each letter is linked to a number;

each number corresponds to an Arcanum;

each Arcanum is the number of an occult power.

The 22 letters of which the keyboard of the language is composed form all the names which,

according to the secret forces symbolized by the letters,

destine the man so named to the vicissitudes which we define by

the vulgar terms of *luck* and *misfortune*."[9]

—Count Alessandro Cagliostro

313

<u>Invocation of Osiris</u>

"I am Osiris Onnophris who is found perfect

before the Gods.

I hath said:

These are the elements of my Body perfected

through suffering,

glorified through trial.

The scent of the dying Rose is as the repressed sigh

of my Suffering.

And the flame-red Fire as the energy of mine

undaunted Will.

And the Cup of Wine is the pouring out of

the blood of my heart,

sacrificed unto Regeneration,

unto the newer life.

And the bread and salt are as the foundations of my body,

which I destroy in order that they may be renewed.

For I am Osiris Triumphant.
Even Osiris Onnophris
the Justified One.
I am He who is clothed with the body of flesh
yet in whom flames the spirit of the eternal Gods.
I am the Lord of Life.
I am triumphant over Death,
and whosoever partaketh with me shall with me arise.
I am the manifester in Matter of Those
whose abode is the Invisible.
I am the purified. I stand upon the Universe.
I am it's Reconciler with the eternal Gods.
I am the Perfector of Matter, and without me the
Universe is not."[10]

—Osiris Onnophris, ancient king of Egypt

"On one of these days it happened,
when the king's son Tuthmosis had arrived on his journey
about the time of mid-day,
and had stretched himself to rest in the shade of this great god,
that sleep overtook him.
He dreamt in his slumber at the moment when the sun was
at the zenith,
and it seemed to him as though this great god spoke to him
with his own mouth,
just as a father speaks to his son, addressing him thus:

'Behold me, look at me, thou, my son Tuthmosis.
I am your father Horemkhu, Kheper, Ra, Tmu.
The kingdom shall be given to you .... and you shall wear
the white crown and the red crown on the throne of the earth-
god Seb, the youngest among the gods. The world shall
be yours in its length and in its breadth,

as far as the light of the eye of the lord of the universe shines.

Plenty and riches shall be yours;

the best from the interior of the land,

and rich tributes from all nations;

long years shall be granted to you as your term of life.

My countenance is gracious towards you,

and my heart clings to you;

I will give you the best of all things.

The sand of the district in which I have my existence

has covered me up.

Promise me that you will do what I wish in my heart;

then shall I know whether you are my son,

my helper.

Go forward let me be united to you. I am . . . '

After this Tuthmosis awoke,

and he repeated all these speeches,

and he understood the meaning of the words of the god

and laid them up in his heart,

speaking thus with himself:

I see how the dwellers in the temple of the city honour this
god with sacrificial gifts without thinking of freeing from sand
the work of King Khaf-Ra,
the statue which was made to Tmu-Horemkhu."[1]

The remaining lines of text have been lost. History tells
us that prince Tuthmosis became King Tuthmosis 4th.

—The Tuthmosis 4th Dream Stele

"Let us make an image of the soul that may have his own

words presented before his eyes.

Of what sort?

An ideal image of the soul,

like the composite creations of ancient mythology,

such as the Chimera or Scylla or Cerberus,

and there are many others in which two or more different

natures are said to grow into one.

There are said of have been such unions.

Then do you now model the form of a multitudinous,

many-headed monster,

having a ring of heads of all manner of beasts,

tame and wild,

which he is able to generate and metamorphose at will.

You suppose marvellous powers in the artist;

but as language is more pliable than wax or any similar

substance,

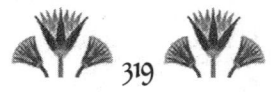

let there be such a model as you propose.

Suppose now that you make a second form as of a lion,

and a third of a man,

the second smaller than the first,

and the third smaller than the second.

That, he said, is an easier task;

and I have made them as you say.

And now join the,

and let the three grow into one.

That has been accomplished.

Next fashion the outside of them into a single image,

as of a man,

so that he who is not able to look within,

and sees only the outer hull,

may believe the beast to be a single human creature.

I have done so, he said.

And now,

to him who maintains that it is profitable for the human

creature to be unjust, and unprofitable to be just,

let us reply that, if he be right,

it is profitable for this creature to feast the multitudinous

monster and strengthen the lion and the lion-like qualities,

but to starve and weaken the man,

who is consequently liable to be dragged about at the mercy of

either of the other two;

and he is not to attempt to familiarize or harmonize them

with one another-

- he ought rather to suffer them to fight and bite and devour

one another."[12]

—Plato
Republic, Book IX

"De dracone, quae est aquila, serpens, scorpion.

Threefold is the nature of life,

eagle,

serpent,

and scorpion.

And of these the scorpion is he that,

having no lion of light and of courage within him,

seemeth to himself encircled by fire,

and driving his stinger into himself,

he dieth.

Such are the black brothers, that cry:

I am I,

they that deny love,

restricting it to their own nature.

But the serpent is the secret nature of man,

that is life and death,

and maketh his way through the generations in silence.

And he eagle is that might of life

Which is the key of magick,

unlifting the body and its appurtenance unto high ecstacy

upon his wings.

It is by virtue thereof that the sphinx beholdeth the sun

unwinking,

and confronteth the pyramid without shame.

Our dragon, therefore,

combining the natures of the eagle and the serpent,

is our love,

the organ of our will,

by those who virtue we perform the work and miracle

of the one substance,

as saith thine ancestor Hermes Trismegistus,

in his tablet of Smaragda.

And this dragon,

is called thy silence,

because in the hour of his operation that within thee which

saith,

ℑ is abolished in its conjunction with the beloved.

For this cause also is its letter nun,

which in our rota is the trump death;

and nun hath the value of fifty,

the number of the gates of understanding."[13]

—Aleister Crowley
Liber Aleph

"See now our sphinx,

with what subility and art is she made whole!

Here is thy light, the lion, the necessity of thy nature,

fortified by thy life, the bill, the power of words,

and guided by thy liberty, the name,

the wit to adapt action to environment.

These are three virtues in one,

necessary to all proper motion,

as I may say in a figure,

the lust of the archer,

the propulsive force of his arm,

and the equilibrating and directing control of his eye.

Of these three if one fail, the mark is not hit.

But hold! Is not a fourth element essential in the work?

Yea, soothly, all were vain without the engine,

arrow and bow.

This engine is thy body,

possessed by thee and used by thee for thy work,

yet not part of thee,

even as are his weapons to this archer in my similitude.

Thus is thy dragon to be cherished of thy lion,

but if thou lack energy and endurance of thy bull,

thy tools lie idle, and if cunning and intelligence,

with experience also of thy man,

thy shaft flieth crooked.

So then,

O my son, do thou perfect thyself in these four powers,

and that with equity....

Now then at last art thou made ready to confront the

pyramid,

If thou art established as a sphinx.

For it also hath he foursquare base of law,

and the four triangles of light,

life, love and liberty for its sides,

that meet in a point of perfection that is hadith,

poised to the kiss of nuith.

But in this pyramid there is no difference of

form between the sides,

as it is in thy sphinx,

for these are wholly one, save in direction.

Thou art then in harmony of the four by right of thy

attainment of adeptship,

the crown of thy manhood,

but not an identity, as in godhead.

Therefore may it be said from one point of sight

that thine achievement is but a preparation,

an adornment of the bride for the temple of hymen,

and his rite.

Verily,

O my son,

327

I deem in my wisdom that his whole work of thy
development to sphinxhood cometh before the work
of theurgy,
for the lord descendeth not upon a temple ill-conceived,
and builded wry,
nor abideth in a shrine unworthy.
Accomplish then this task in patience, with assiduity,
not hasting furiously after godliness.
For this is most sure,
that to the beauty of a maiden answereth
the lust of her lord,
spontaneous and without effort
or appeal of her contriving."[14]

—Aleister Crowley
Liber Aleph part 7

"Freud dismissed Jung's concept of a 'collective unconscious' and offered instead his own idea of archaic inheritance.

According to Freud,

Moses was an Egyptian,

who gave to the Jews the religion of monotheism,

and was murdered in the wilderness....

'The founding of the Mohammedan religion seems to me to be an abbreviated repetition of the Jewish one,'

Freud wrote,

but Islam 'lacked the profundity which the Jewish religion resulted from the murder of its founder.'"[15]

—Sigmund Freud
Moses and Monotheism

"Assuming all of that is true,
researchers believe that a logical location for the biblical
Red Sea is modern-day Lake Sirbonis.
According to a Bulletin Of The American
Meteorological Society account,
computer calculations indicate that because of the peculiar
geography of the northern end of the Red Sea,
a moderate wind blowing constantly for about 10 hours
could have caused the sea to recede about a mile
and the water level to drop 10 ft.,
leaving dry land for a period of time
before crashing back when the winds died down."[16]

—Mike Fillon
Science Solves the Ancient Mysteries of the Bible

"...Osiris,

God of vegetation and cycles.

Osiris is very earthy,

compare the Capricorn birth of Christ.

Osiris is also a Christ-figure, who,

though murdered by Typhon,

cut to pieces and his bones scattered in the Nile,

yet was reassembled and born again.

Osiris, in short, is the Conquest of Death,

whereas Horus, in a more subtle sense,

is the understanding that Life and Death are equivalent.

Vita quidem nomen vita, opus autem mors est."[17]

—Osiris Onnophris
Occultopedia

"Behdet,

Egypt's northernmost city,

the city of Horus, became in Arabic,

Baghdad." [18]

—E. E. Rehmus
The Magician's Dictionary

"The Great Pyramid was dedicated to the god
Hermes,

the personification of Universal Wisdom;

it was not only a temple of initiation

but a repository for the secret truths

which he calls the foundation of all the arts and sciences.

The time will come,...

when the secret Wisdom shall again be the dominating religious

and philosophical urge of the world:

'Out of the cold ashes of lifeless creeds,

shall rise phoenix-like the ancient Mysteries....

The unfolding of man's spiritual nature is as much an exact

science as astronomy, medicine and jurisprudence.'"[19]

—Manly P. Hall
Freemasonry and the Ancient Egyptians

333

"The Book of the Dead,

though it appears to be a ritual for funerary rites of a

deceased king or high official, was actually a description of

the trials, temptations and difficulties

which the adept had to meet and overcome as he progressed

from knowledge to knowledge and from power to power,

as he penetrated the superphysical regions

from plane to plane.

The ultimate goal of initiation, was 'full realization of the

essential divine nature of man,

the recovery by the individual of the full knowledge and

powers of his divine spiritual nature,

of that which he is now dead through the 'Fall of Man'

into matter and physical life.'"[20]

—William Kingsland, The Great Pyramid in
Fact and in Theory

334

"The Egyptians,
who produced the first true writing system almost
simultaneously with the Sumerians of lower Mesopotamia,
ascribe their invention of the hieroglyphics to
ibis-headed Thoth.
Islamic lore tells how Allah secretly gave the alphabet
to Adam,
while the Talmud lists writing as one of the things created
in the twilight of Sabbath eve."[21]

—Tod Harris
The Word Made Flesh

"My mouth is opened by Ptah

and what was on my mouth has been loosened

by my local god.

Thoth comes indeed,

filled and equipped with magic,

And the bonds of Seth which restricted my mouth have

been loosened.

Atum has warded them off and has cast away the

restrictions of Seth.

My mouth is opened,

my mouth is split open by Shu.

And that iron harpoon of his which he split open the mouths

of the gods.

I am Sekhmet,

and I sit beside Her who is in the great wind of the sky;

I am Orion the Great,
who dwells with the Souls of Heliopolis.
As for any magic spell
or any words which may be uttered against me,
the gods will rise up against it,
even the entire Ennead."[22]

–The Egyptian Book of the Dead
The Papyrus of Ani

"The Greeks identified Thoth with their god Hermes,

and they credited him with inventing astronomy and

astrology,

the science of numbers and mathematics,

geometry and land surveying, medicine, and botany.

Also, they believed he was the first to organize religion and

government,

and to establish rules concerning the worship of gods.

He was said to have composed hymns, prayers, and

liturgical works, and to have invented numbers, the alphabet,

reading, writing, and oratory.

In short, he was the author of every branch of knowledge,

both human and divine."[23]

—Anthony S. Mercatante
Who's Who in Egyptian Mythology

338

"The Emerald Tablets of Thoth –
The Atlantean

is a literal translation and interpretation of one of the

most ancient and secret of the

Great Works of the Ancient World.

The history of the tablets translated in the following pages

is strange and beyond the belief of modern scientists.

Their antiquity is stupendous,

dating back some 36,000 years BC.

The writer is Thoth,

an Atlantean Priest-King,

who founded a colony in ancient Egypt after the sinking of

the mother country.

He was the builder of the Great Pyramid of Giza,

erroneously attributed to Cheops.

In it he incorporated his knowledge of the ancient wisdom
and also securely secreted records and instruments of
ancient Atlantis.
For some 16,000 years,
he ruled the ancient race of Egypt,
from approximately 50,000 BC to 36,000 BC.
At that time,
the ancient barbarous race among which he and his followers
had settled had been raised to a high degree of civilization....

They consist of twelve tablets of emerald green,
formed from a substance created through
alchemical transmutation.
They are imperishable,
resistant to all elements and substances.
In effect,
the atomic and cellular structure is fixed,

no change ever taking place....
Upon them are engraved characters in the
ancient Atlantean language....

The tablets are fastened together with hoops of golden
colored alloy suspended from a rod of the same material...."[24]

—Dr. Doreal
The Emerald Tablets, Preface

"I, Thoth, the Atlantean,

give of my wisdom,

give of my knowledge,

give of my power.

Freely I give to the children of men.

Give that they, too, might have wisdom to shine through the

world from the veil of the night."[25]

—Thoth
Emerald Tablet No. 1, The History of Thoth,
The Atlantean

"That every man to whom with God's permission
the mysteries of future time are revealed
may uphold Good and triumph over Evil
by the wise direction of the mind and will."[26]

—Hermes-Thoth
Hundred Aphorisms

"Hermes-Thoth was the creator of philosophy. He was also known as Atlas and Enoch."[27]

–Sir James George Frazer
The Golden Bough

"...Into the spaceship

I brought all my records,

brought the records of sunken Atlantis.

Gathered I all of my powers,

instruments many of mighty magic....

Deep neath the rocks,

I buried my spaceship,

Waiting the time When man might be free.

Over the spaceship,

erected a marker in the form of a lion yet like unto man.

There neath the image rests yet my spaceship,

forth to be brought When need shall arise.

Know ye, O man,

that far in the future,

invaders shall come from out of the deep.

Then awake, ye who have wisdom.

Bring forth my ship and conquer with ease.

Deep neath the image lies my secret.

Search and find in the pyramid I built."[28]

—Thoth
Emerald Tablet No. 5, The Dwellers of Unal

"Thoth,

the god of the scribes

has bestowed upon me the gift of the knowledge of his art.

I have been initiated into the secrets of writing.

I can even read the intricate tablets in Sumerian.

I understand the enigmatic words

in the stone carvings from the days of the Flood."[29]

—King Ashurbanipal of Assyria

347

"None of our thoughts could comprehend the nature

of God,

nor any language define it.

What is incorporeal,

invisible, without form,

cannot be grasped by our senses;

What is eternal cannot be measured by the short rule of time:

God is therefore ineffable.

He is the absolute truth,

The absolute power;

And the unchangeable absolute cannot be comprehended on

this earth."[30]

—Hermes-Thoth
Hundred Aphorisms

"34. Knowledge is the gift of God;
for all Knowledge is unbodily but useth the Mind as an
Instrument,
as the Mind useth the Body."

"37. When that Period was fulfilled,
the bond of all things was loosed and untied by the Will of
God;
for all living Creatures being Hermaphroditical,
or Male and Female,
were loosed and untied together with Man;
and so the Males were apart by themselves and the
Females likewise.
God desires therefore that every man should learn to know
himself for what he is,
and to distinguish his superior and invisible being from the
invisible form,

Which is only the shell.

When he has recognized the duality of his creation,

he no longer allows himself to be seduced by the charm of

impermanent things;

his thought has no other aim but to see and pursue,

across the infinite,

the absolute beauty whose contemplation is the sovereign good

promised to his rehabilitated mind."[31]

—Hermes Trismegistus
Corpus Hermeticum

"Tem,

The oldest of the creation gods in Egyptian mythology,

variously called 'divine god,' 'self-created,'

'maker of the gods,' and 'maker of men.'

According to the Pyramid Text of Pepi I,

Tem existed when: Not was sky, Not was earth,

Not was men, Not were born the gods,

Not was death....

The thoughts of Tem were translated into words by

the god Thoth, who was his mind or intelligence.

When Thoth uttered the words,

all creation came into being."[32]

—Anthony S. Mercatante
Who's Who in Egyptian Mythology

351

"Thoth, Moon god, patron of the arts,

speech,

hieroglyphics,

science and wisdom.

He was called the 'heart of Ra,'

the 'lord of divine words,'

and the 'self-created,'

to whom none hath given birth, god one.

I am Thoth,

the excellent scribe,

whose hands are pure;

the lord of the two horns,

who makes iniquity to be destroyed;

the scribe of right and truth,

who abominates wrongdoing....

I am Thoth,

The lord of right and truth,

Who judges right and truth for the gods;

The judge of words in their essence,

Whose words triumph over violence.

I have scattered the darkness;

I have driven away the whirlwind and the storm;

And I have given the pleasant breeze of the north wind

unto Osiris,

the beautiful being,

as he came forth from the body of her who gave him birth....

...Thoth, the judge of right and truth of the Great

Company of the Gods who are in the presence of Osiris,

saith:

Hear ye this judgment.

The heart of Osiris hath in very truth been weighed,

and his Heart-soul hath borne testimony on his behalf;

his heart hath been found right by the trial

in the Great Balance.

There hath not been found any wickedness in him;

he hath not wasted the offerings which have been made

in the temples;

he hath not committed any evil act;

and he hath not set his mouth in motion with words of evil

whilst he was upon earth."[33]

—The Speech of Thoth
The Pymander

"Desireth thou to know the deep, hidden secret?

Look in thy heart where the knowledge is found.

Know that in thee the secret is hidden,

the source of all life and the source of all death.

List ye, O man, while I tell the secret,

reveal unto thee the secret of old.

Deep in Earth's heart lies the flower,

the source of the Spirit binds all in its form or ye know that

the Earth is living in body as thou art alive in thine own

formed form.

The Flower of Life is as thine own place of Spirit

and streams through the Earth as thine flows through

thy form;

giving of life to the Earth and its children,

renewing the Spirit from form unto form.

This is the Spirit that is form of thy body,

shaping and moulding into its form.

Know ye, O man, that thy form is dual,

balanced in polarity while formed in its form.

Know that when fast on thee Death approaches,

it is only because thy balance is shaken.

It is only because one pole has been lost.

Know that the secret of life in Amenti is the secret of

restoring the balance of poles.

All that exists has form and is living because of the Spirit

of life in its poles.

List ye, O Man, whilst I give the secret so that ye,

too, shalt taste not of change.

One hour each day shalt thou lie with thine head pointed to

the place of the positive, north.

One hour each day shalt they head be pointed to the place

of the negative pole, south.

Whilst they head is placed to the northward,

hold thou thy consciousness from the chest to the head.

And when they head is placed southward,

hold thy thought from chest to the feet.

Hold thou in balance once in each seven,

and thy balance will retain the whole of its strength.

Aye, if thou be old, thy body will freshen and thy strength

will become as a youth's.

This is the secret known to the Masters by which they

hold off the fingers of Death.

Neglect not to follow the path I have shown,

for when thou has passed beyond years to a hundred to neglect

it will mean the coming of Death.

...Learn ye the secret that is Master of Time.

Learn ye how those ye call Masters are able to

remember the lives of the past.

Great is the secret yet easy to master,

giving to thee the mastery of time.

When upon thee death fast approaches,

357

fear not but know ye are the master of Death.

Relax the body, resist not with tension.

Place in thy heart the flame of thy Soul.

Swiftly then sweep it to the seat of the triangle.

Hold it for a moment, then move to the goal.

This, thy goal, is the place between thine eyebrows,

the place where memory of life must hold sway.

Hold thou thy flame here in thy brain-seat until the fingers

of Death grasp thy Soul.

Then as thou pass through the state of transition,

surely the memories of life shall pass, too.

Then shalt the past be as one with the present.

Then shall the memory of all be retained.

Free shalt thou be from all retrogression.

The things of the past will live in today...."[34]

—Thoth, The Keys to Life and Death

358

"...List ye,

O man,

to the deep hidden wisdom,

lost to the world since the time of the Dwellers,

lost and forgotten by men of this age.

Know ye this Earth is but a portal,

guarded by powers unknown to man.

Yet, the Dark Lords hide the entrance that leads to the

Heaven-born land.

Know ye,

the way to the sphere of Arulu is guarded by barriers

opened only to Light-born man.

Upon Earth,

I am the holder of the keys to the gates of the

Sacred Land.

Command I,

by the powers beyond me,

to leave the keys to the world of man.

Before I depart,

I give ye the Secrets of how ye may rise from

the bondage of darkness,

cast off the fetters of flesh that have bound ye,

rise from the darkness to the Light."[35]

—Thoth

Emerald Tablet No. 14, Supplemental

"Shazam is a notariqon of:

S for the wisdom of Solomon;
H for the strength of Hercules;
A for the stamina of Atlas;
Z for the power of Zeus;
A for the courage of Achilles;
M for the speed of Mercury."[36]

—Adventures of Captain Marvel

"Isis,

The Thousand-Named Egyptian Goddess,

whose aspects are also the cow-headed Hathor

and the hippopotamus goddess,

Taurt

the first deity of magic.

Mother and wife of Osiris.

She was originally a mortal sorceress who desired

to become a goddess.

From some of Ra's spittle

she fashioned a viper of clay,

which she then brought to life and caused to bite

and poison him.

She released its antidote to him only when he agreed to tell

her his secret names.

The power thereof was so great that it ignited her

deification.

Ra has at least three names:

Khepera, Ra and Atum,
Morning, Noon and Sunset.
At night,
he is Osiris and his eye is Thoth,
the moon, as his eye by day is the Sun....

Ra's secret name was heard only by Isis herself,
and she has never deigned to share with anyone else.
It is for this reason that she is identified as
the Goddess of Mystery itself....

The understanding of these names, indeed,
is the key to all Egyptian wisdom,
for sooner or later,
all the Gods run into and become one another.

363

As we have begun to suspect,
the secret of magic is the knowledge that everything
is everything else.
Isis is the Goddess of Ultimate Mystery itself
and the Mother of all Magick.
She is the great veil over the night that none may remove.
She represents the manifest world,
as Nephthys is the unmanifest."[37]

— The Goddess Isis, Occultopedia

The Doctrine of Apollonius

"I studied in my long journeys the wisdom of all countries.

All the philosophic sects appeared before me,

wearing the ornaments each had created for itself,

and I retired into the solitude and dignity of my being to

consider my choice.

All seemed to me beautiful in their own ways,

And of a superhuman appearance;

Some insinuated themselves into my reason with seductive

graces and attempted to capture me with marvelous promises.

One announced to me that,

cradled and rocked in its dreams,

I should see descend upon me the swarming pleasures of a

voluptuous life;

Another did not pride itself on sparing me the sorrows of life

but it offered,

at the end of these trials,

365

a perpetual blissful quietude.

Yet another offered me the soul in perfect equilibrium
between good and evil;
and still another encouraged me to venture everything in order
to find happiness.

All agreed in binding me to earth by why they called the
legitimate satisfactions of the material half of my being.

Only one of these forms of wisdom, the Egyptian,
kept itself aloof, silent and reserved.

It appeared last of all, when it saw that its companions had
not succeeded in capturing me.

'Young man,' it said to me,
'I am the daughter of the past and the mother of the future;
I am the queen of the spirits and God's reflection on earth
and in all the worlds.

366

To be admitted into my empire,

you must renounce the vanities of earth,

sensual delicacies and the pride of life.

I forbid love to my disciples as a dangerous madness

of the soul,

and I command their silence so that they may always feel

themselves in the presence of God.

I abhor bloody sacrifices that suppose in the Supreme

Being the ferocity of a tyrant,

and I teach filial prayers which are,

the offering of incense,

the only cult worthy of the Father of all things.

If you have the courage to follow me to the heights where

Truth abides I shall make a new man of you;

I shall give you new eyes which shall be opened upon the

infinite world of immortal essences.

367

You shall measure time with a single glance;

you shall embrace all beings as one,

in a single thought;

the divine powers shall reveal their secrets to you and the

forces of nature shall obey you.'

In this manner was I addressed by the wisdom of Egypt,

the great Magic of the sons of God:

I followed it, and it has kept its promises to me."[38]

—Apollonius of Tyana
The Doctrine of Apollonius

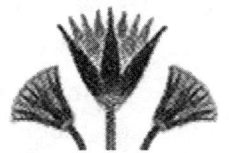

Illustrations

Front cover background photograph is a halftone rendition of the painting *The Golden Bough* by the British artist Joseph Mallord William Turner (1775-1851), which title was taken from an incident in the *Aeneid*. —Courtesy Tate Britain and Wikipedia Encyclopedia.

Back cover photographs of Thoth courtesy of the Canadian Museum of Civilization. Oannes, also known as Ea, Enki, and Poseidon, pottery statuette thought to have been found at Nineveh. —Robert Temple's *The Sirius Mystery*, 1997, Fig. 35; Isis and Osiris (Serapis) stele photograph courtesy of the Higher Council of Water Beings. More information and the historical records of water-beings can be found at the website www.water-consciousness.com.

Figure 1. The god Ea in the water *apsũ*. "Ea was an amphibious, heavenly Water-Being represented in an Assyrian cylinder seal was also known as Enki, Oannes, and Poseidon. In later traditions, such as the Philistines, the Fish-Tailed God was called, Dagon, which is mentioned in the Bible. Ea was the later Akkadian name for Enki, the main God of the Sumerian City of Eridu. This Fish-Tailed God was worshipped off the coast of Syria and appears in Babylonian cylinder seals, in Persian coins, in Etruscan

amphoras, in Phoenician coins, on Greco-Phoenician scarabs, and in the reliefs of the Palace of Sargon. The story in which Enki/Oannes tells the Sumerian Noah 'Uta-Napishtim' to build an ark, is much the same as the Bible's version of the great disaster. Many ancient legends portray this *Fisher King* as having saved mankind from the Great Flood. Some texts suggest that Ea lived at the bottom of the Apsu, or Abyss in fresh water. Berossus describes Enki/Oannes as 'He of the vast intellect,' 'Lord of the Sacred Eye,' 'God of Wisdom.' He is said to have emerged four times, at long intervals, from the subterranean ocean to teach men the arts of civilization. When he appears, it is in human form wearing a fish-tailed cloak. After educating mankind he returns to the waters as darkness falls." —Dr. Lilliana Corredor and Members of the Higher Council of Water Beings. More information is available at the *Historical Records of Water Beings* at the website www.water-consciousness.com.

Figure 2. The Legend of St. George and the Dragon. "St. George journeyed for many months by land and sea until he came to Egypt. Here he met a poor hermit who told him that everyone in that land was in great distress, for a dragon had long ravaged the country. 'Every day,' said the old man, 'he demands the sacrifice of a beautiful maiden and now all the young girls have been killed. The King's daughter alone remains, and unless we can find a knight who can slay the dragon she will be sacrificed tomorrow. The king of Egypt will give his daughter in marriage to the champion who overcomes this terrible monster.'" — Courtesy http://www.woodlands-junior.kent.sch.uk.

Figure 3. Map of Atlantis (1655). This is a copy of the original map of Atlantis from Atanasius Kircher's (1601-1680) atlas titled *Terra Mundas Subterraneous* printed in 1665. The Latin inscription on the top left hand corner of the map of Atlantis translates: "Site of Atlantis now beneath the sea according to the beliefs of the Egyptians and the description of Plato."

Figure 4. Painting of the mythical harbor of Atlantis. Courtesy of *Occultopedia, An Encyclopedia of Occultism and the Unexplained,* website designed by Marcus Gay at http://www.occultopedia.com.

Figure 5. Ur-Nippur Tablet. "The exhibit are samples of the 'Flood Mud' discovered beneath Ur, and the Nippur Tablet, a clay tablet from ancient Nippur which is the only surviving document of the Sumerian flood story, dating from the 17th century BC. Written in Sumerian, it not only tells the flood story, but also describes the creation of humans and animals, and records the names of antediluvian cities and their rulers.

Archaeologists and language specialists today doubt that the Ur (or Kish) floods could be the source of the Mesopotamian flood narratives. Instead, they view the discovered flood deposits merely as evidence that flooding was a persistent hazard in the flat alluvial plain of southern Mesopotamia. On the other hand, many scholars believe that the Mesopotamian flood tradition was reshaped by Hebrew writers of the 8th and 6th centuries BC into the biblical account of Noah and the Great Deluge found in the Book of Genesis." —Courtesy The McClung Museum at http://www.mcclungmuseum.utk.edu.

Figure 6. A Medieval Hebrew Bible manuscript scroll, known as *The Masoretic Text*. —Courtesy *The Dead Sea Exhibit to the Forbidden Book* website at www.deadsea exhibit.org. "The Hebrew word *mesorah* (הרוסמ) refers to the transmission of a tradition. In fact, in a very broad sense it can refer to the entire chain of Jewish tradition. But in terms of the **masoretic text** the word *mesorah* has a very specific meaning: it refers to concise marginal notes in manuscripts (and later printings) of the Hebrew Bible which note textual details, usually about the precise spelling of words." —*Free Definition* website at www.free-definition.com/masoretic_text.html.

Figure 7. Map of the Earliest Civilizations. —Courtesy *FlashVIC*, Inc. website at http://www.virtual-egypt.com.

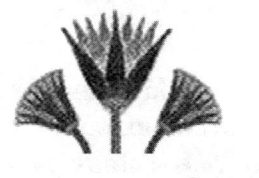

Consulted Works

I have endeavored to supply the reader with the fundamental information needed to find the quoted authors. On some occasion I have elaborated more than is necessary regarding some of the more interesting facts about their life, literary works, and place in society. The majority of sources are available in print and on the Internet.

Chapter 1 - Ancient Wisdom, Great Knowledge & Mystical Experiences   21

1. Benjamin Disraeli (1804-1881). British politician and prime minister in 1868. This quotation can be found at the *Quotations Page*, website http://www.quotations page.com.
2. Kamal Jumblatt (1917-1977). Interview in <u>Le Jour</u>, March 31, 1967. Kamal Jumblatt was the Lebanese president-elect and the Druze leader. He was assassinated in 1977. *See* http://en.freedictionary.com.
3. Winston Churchill (1874-1965). *See* website at http://en.free dictionary.com.
4. Roger Bacon, (1211-1292). Henry Thomas and Dana Lee Thomas' *Living Biographies of Great Scientists*.

Illustrations by Gordon Ross. Garden City, NY: Blue Ribbons Books, 1946, pp. 13-20.

5. Marsilio Ficino. *See* Tobias Churton's *The Gnostics*. Barnes and Noble Books, New York, 1987, p. 106. "15th century philosopher best known for having translated Plato and the Neoplatonists, as well as Hermes Trismegistus. He thought that the world was an 'emanation of God' and that one could draw heavenly influences by simply meditating on the planets."—E. E. Rehmus, *The Magician's Dictionary: An Apocalyptic Cyclopaedia of Advanced Ma/magi (Kal Arts and Alternate Meanings)*, Feral House, 1990 (out of print).

6. James the Just. Quotation from Tobias Churton's *The Gnostics*. Barnes and Noble Books, New York, 1987, pp. 3-32. James the Just says of Jesus, *The First Apocalypse of James*. A passage that describes a discussion between Jesus and James the Just, both before and after the Crucifixion. James says he is concerned for Jesus but Jesus says the Crucifixion was in reality, only an appearance, and that he is glorified by it, not degraded.

7. Publilius Syrus, (42 BC). Quoted from John Bartlett, comp. 1919. *Familiar Quotations*, 10th ed. *See* website at http://www.columbia.edu. Pubililus (less correctly Publius) Syrus, a Latin writer of mimes who flourished in the 1st century BC. He was a native of Syria and was brought as a slave to Italy, but by his wit he won the favor of his master, who freed and educated him.

8. Lord Francis Bacon, (1561-1626). *The Essays; Counsels, Civil and Moral of Francis Bacon*. A. L. Burk Company Publishers, New York, 1905, p. 324.

(First Edition 1597). Including also his apophthegms, elegant sentences, and wisdom from the ancients.

9. Publius Vergilius "Vergil" Maro, (70-19 BC). *Vergil on the Celestial Virtues* quoted in 1651, translation of Henry Cornelius Agrippa's *Three Books of Occult Philosophy*, 1531, p. 3. Quotation found in Tobias Churton's *The Gnostics*. Barnes and Noble Books, New York, 1987.

10. *Whales,* E. E. Rehmus, *The Magician's Dictionary*: *An Apocalyptic Cyclopaedia of Advanced Ma/magi (Kal Arts and Alternate Meanings)*, Feral House, 1990. *See* website at http://www.chronozon.com.

11. Nesta Webster, *Secret Societies and Subversive Movements*, London, Boswell, 1924. More information on the secret societies of the early 20's can be can be found at *The Grand Lodge of British Columbia and Yukon* at website http://www.freemasonry.bcy.ca.

12. *Die neresten Arbeiten des Spartacusund Philo in dem Illuminaten* – Orden, 1794, p. 165. *See Nesta Webster* at http://www.ca.geocities.com.

13. Artephius (200-1119) also known as Apollonius of Tyana and possibly the Arabic poet and alchemist Al "Toghari" who died around 1119. *The Secret Book.* "A well known supporter of Hermetic philosophy who is said to have died in the early 12th century, and declared to have lived a thousand years by means of alchemical secrets. Francois Pic mentioned that in opinions of certain servant Artephius was identical with Apollonius of Tyana, who was born in the first century by that name and died in the 12th as Artephius. Many extravagant and curious works are said to have been written by Artephius: *De Vita Propaganda* (The Art of

375

Prolonging Life) which he comments in the preface that he is writing it when 125 years old; *The Key to Supreme Wisdom*; a book on the character of the planets; a book on the significance of the songs of birds; on things of past and future; and on the Philosopher's Stone. A neo-Pythagorean of Greece who acquired a reputation for his magical powers. He is considered a contemporary of Christ. Francis Barrett claimed him to be 'one of the most extraordinary persons that ever appeared in the world.' Born at Tyana, in Asia Minor, he was educated at Tarsus, and at the Temple of Aesculapius at Aegae, where at sixteen he became an adherent of Pythagoras whose discipline he ascribed to all of his life. He died during the second century AD. In his desire for knowledge he traveled many Eastern countries and according to legend he performed miracles where ever he went. One legend has it that an Indian magician made seven rings representing the seven planets and presented them to Apollonius who wore a different one each day. It is said this enabled him to maintain his youthful vigor well into old age. He is reputed to have lived to be one thousand years old. Apollonius' death is a mystery. According to some he fell out of favor with Emperor Severu, who put him on trial and had his hair cut off to eliminate his magical powers. Apollonius simply disappeared from the courtroom never to be seen again." *See* the website *The Alchemy Web Site* at http://www. Levity.com.

14. Mark Twain (1835-1910). Born Samuel L. Clemens. *See* http://www.twainquotes.com by Barbara Schmitd.

15. Gary K. North, *None Dare Call It Witchcraft*, New Rochelle: Arlington House, 1967.
16. *Psalm* 46, KJV, *The Holy Bible*.
17. Helena P. Blavatsky (1831-1891), *The Secret Doctrine*, 1888. A Russian born American mystic and cofounder of the Theosophical Society in New York in 1873. Blavatsky exhibited psychic powers at an early age, and claimed to perform acts of mediumship, levitation, telepathy and clairvoyance. Her writings include *Isis Unveiled* (1877) and *The Secret Doctrine,* 1888.
18. Iamblichus (250–330). *Treatise On the [Egyptian] Mysteries.* The true title of this treaty is: *Answer of master Abammon to a letter sent by Porphyry to Anebon and solution of the difficulties which can be found there.* The subtitle *De mysteriis Aegyptiorum* (On the Egyptian Mysteries) can be found in a secondary manuscript and was adopted instead if the true title by the first translators: Marsile Ficin (Venice, 1497), and Nicolas Scutellius (Rome, 1556). Iamblichus, the Neoplatonic magus (250-325) of whom Julian the Apostate said, "He is posterior to Plato only in time, not in genius." Author of *On the Mysteries of the Egyptians, Chaldeans and Assyrians*, which is the foundation of Cabalism. It was Iamblichus, also, who popularized Proclus. More information can be found at *The Encyclopedia of the Goddess Athena* at the website http://www.goddess-athena.org.
19. Sir Arthur Charles Clark (1917-2001). A British science fiction writer who in 1968 collaborated with filmmaker Stanley Kubrick in *2001: A Space Odyssey. Columbia Electronic Encyclopedia,* 6th ed.
20. Bene Gesserit, *Axioms. See* http://www.eifuki.co.uk.

21. Ashok K. Gangadean, *The Quest for the Primal Word. What is the origin of language?* Parabola: The Magazine of Myth and Tradition, Vol. 20, No. 3, August 1995, p. 44. Dr. Gangadean is a professor of Philosophy at Haverford College, PA.

22. Dr. Doreal, Brotherhood of the Great White Temple. *Interpretation of the Book of Revelation*, Verse 13:18, p. 33. *See* website at http://www.bwtemple.org.

23. Howard Schwartz, *How the Tenth Tribe Lost Its Words.* Reprinted from *Adams Soul: The Collected Tales of Howard Schwartz*, Northvale, N.J.: Jason Aronson, 1992. *See* Parabola: The Magazine of Myth and Tradition, Vol. 20, No. 3, August 1995, p. 83.

24. Ross Fuller, *On Listening and the Word. The teachings of the Desert Fathers. See* Parabola: The Magazine of Myth and Tradition, Vol. 20, No. 3, August 1995, pp. 33-38.

25. Pope Saint Gregory "the Great" (540-604). *See* http://www.newadvent.com.

26. Michael Angelo (1746-1801). *See* http://encyclopedia. freedictionary.com.

27. Benjamin Disraeli. See *Quotations Page,* at http://www.quotationpage.com.

28. René A. Schwaller De Lubicz, *Sacred Silence*, Rochester: Inner Traditions International, 1988, pp. 167-68. "René Schwaller de Lubicz (1887–1961) is known to English readers primarily for his work in uncovering the spiritual and cosmological insights of ancient Egypt. In books like *Esotericism and Symbol, The Temple in Man, Symbol and the Symbolic, The Egyptian Miracle*, and the monumental *The Temple of*

Man--whose long awaited English translation has finally appeared--Schwaller de Lubicz argued, among other things, that Egyptian civilization is much older than orthodox Egyptologists suggest, a claim receiving renewed interest through the recent work of Graham Hancock and Robert Bauval."—Gary Lachman. *Theosophical Society in America.*

29. Plato (427-347 BC), *Republic* VI 508. *See* http://www.friesian.com/plato.htm.

30. Abraham Cohen, *Everyman's Talmud, The Major Teachings of the Rabbinic Sages*, New York: E. P. Dutton. 1949, III. Dietetics, p. 246-47. Dietetics and the importance of diet in the preservation of health was recognized by the Rabbis and the *Talmud* has many passages which treat articles of food as wholesome, or otherwise. Bread seems to have been literally the staff of life.

31. Plato (427-347 BC), *Timaeus*. Plato offers one version of the answer through the words of an Egyptian priest.

32. Count Alessandro Cagliostro (1743-1795). Born Giuseppe Balsamo, charlatan, magician, and adventurer who enjoyed enormous success in Parisian high society in the years preceding the French Revolution. Excerpt from Paul Christian (1811-1877), *The History and Practice of Magic*, NJ: Citadel, 1972. French occultist best known for his *Histoire de la Magie* (1870). He regarded the *Book of Thoth* as containing, in its 22 arcana, "The Science of Will, the principle of all wisdom and the source of all power." Originally published as *Histoire de la magie, du monde surnaturel et de la fatalité à travers les temps et les peuples.*

33. U. S. Andersen, *Three Magic Words: The Key to Power, Peace & Plenty.* Wilshire Books, 1980. ISBN: 0879801654. Is book is out of print.

34. Honoré de Balzac, *The Magic Skin*, New York: Charles Scribner's Sons, 1914. Honoré de Balzac, a French journalist (1799-1850) and writer, regarded as one of the creators of realism in literature. Balzac's huge production of novels and short stories are collected under the name *La Comédie Humaine.*

35. Count Alessandro Cagliostro (1743-1795). *See* Paul Christian, *The History and Practice of Magic.* NJ: Citadel Press, 1972, p. 220. See more information above.

36. A. Saint-Yves d'Alveydre (1842-1909), *Mission de l'Inde en Europe,* Paris, Calmann Lévy, 1886, pp. 54 and 65. *See* website http://www.foundation.bw.

37. Helena P. Blavatsky (1831-1891), *The Secret Doctrine*, 1888. This is an excerpt from the fourth part of a six-part series on the races of mankind, collated from *The Secret Doctrine.* Madame Blavatsky one of the foremost psychic seers of the 19th century.

38. Elsa-Berita Titchenell, *The Masks of Odin*, Pasadena, Ca.: Theosophical University Press, 1985. The *Völuspá* tells the story of Ragnarök, the fall of the Norse gods and the World Tree Yggdrasil and the giants of the Third Race.

39. Sir C. Leonard Woolley, *The Sumerians*, W.W. Norton, London: 1965, p. 20.

40. *Oannes and the Origins of Western Civilization* are taken from a history of Mesopotamia written in the third century BC, by Berossus. Berossus, a third

century Babylonian priest whose work survives only in fragments recorded by later Greek historians. Berossus, from *Ancient Fragments* (Isaac Preston Cory) from V. Pakhomov, 1999.

41. Walter Baucum, *Tracing Dan*, Part 2 Chapter 2. *See* http://www.uhcg.org/Lost-10-Tribes/tracingdan5. html.

42. Helena P. Blavatsky (1831-1891), *The Secret Doctrine*, 1888.

43. William Shakespeare (1564-1616). *See* website http://encyclopedia.freedictionary.com.

44. *Corpus Hermeticum.* Quotation from Tobias Churton's *The Gnostics*, Barnes and Noble Books, New York, 1987, p. 108. This is how the reader first enters the *Corpus Hermeticum. See also* Henry Cornelius Agrippa's *Three Books of Occult Philosophy*, 1531.

45. Charles F. Berlitz, *The Bermuda Triangle*, Doubleday, 1974.

46. Plotinus (204-270). Plotinus is considered to be the founder of Neo-Platonism. He developed a complex spiritual cosmology involving three hypostases: One, Intelligence, and the Soul. Quotation from Tobias Churton's *The Gnostics*, Barnes and Noble Books, New York, 1987, p. 33.

47. *Libellus X.* 24b-25, *Corpus Hermeticum.* Quotation from Tobias Churton's *The Gnostics*, Barnes and Noble Books, New York, 1987, p. 44.

48. Saint Augustine, *Civitas Dei*, XVIII. 29. Quoted in Tobias Churton's *The Gnostics,* Barnes and Noble Books, New York, 1987, p. 105.

49. S. Paul Burholt, *Sacred Threshold. History, eternity, and the Incarnation.* Parabola: The Magazine of Myth and Tradition, Vol. 23, No. 1, 1998, p. 61.

50. Gaius Julius Caesar (100-44 BC). *See Metareligion* at website http://www.metareligion.com.
51. Tod Harris, *The Word Made Flesh. The roots of written language.* Parabola: The Magazine of Myth and Tradition, Vol. 20, No. 3, August 1995, p. 16.
52. Helena P. Blavatsky, *The Races of Man(1) i: Origins*, Theosophy Magazine, Vol. 66, No. 7, 1978.
53. Quoting Nikolaus Copernicus (1473-1543), from Henry Thomas and Dana Lee Thomas' *Living Biographies of Great Scientists.* Blue Ribbons Books, Garden City, New York, 1946, pp. 22-32.
54. Lord Francis Bacon (1573-1625), *The Essays; Counsels, Civil and Moral of Francis Bacon*, NY: A. L. Burk Company Publishers, 1905, pp. 418. (First Edition 1597). Including also his apophthegms, elegant sentences, and wisdom from the ancients.
55. F. Sherwood Taylor. Distinguished historian of alchemy. *See* http://www.levity.com/alchemy.htm.
56. Roger Bacon (1212-1292), Franciscan monk, philosopher, scientist, teacher. *See* website at http://www.levity.com/alchemy/rbacon html.
57. *Proverbs* 1:6-7, KJV, *The Holy Bible.*
58. *Matthew* 13:34-35, KJV, *The Holy Bible.*
59. *Luke* 8:9-10, KJV, *The Holy Bible.*
60. E. E. Rehmus, *Wudjat, Eye of Ra, The Magician's Dictionary: An Apocalyptic Cyclopaedia of Advanced Ma/magi (Kal Arts and Alternate Meanings)*, Feral House, 1990. (out of print).
61. Ithell Colquhoun. Brilliant surreal painter and poet. *See* website at http://www.ithellcolquhoun.co.uk.

62. Michael Maier, *Atalanta Fugiens*, Oppenheim, De Bry. First published in 1671. A copy can be found at *The Alchemy Web Site*, at website http://www.levity. com.

63. Helena P. Blavatsky, *The Secret Doctrine,* 1888. *See* http://www.blavatsky.net.

64. *Seasons of the Moon*, Iyar 5759, April 16, 1999-May 15, 1999. This information can be found at http://www.ohr.org.il and http://philologos.org.

65. Grant Jeffery, *The Signature of God. See* website at http://philologos.org/bpr/files/n009.htm.

66. *Slyphs,* E. E. Rehmus, *The Magician's Dictionary*: *An Apocalyptic Cyclopaedia of Advanced Ma/magi (Kal Arts and Alternate Meanings)*, Feral House, 1990.

67. Socrates and Glaucon. Plato's *Republic. See Sacred Text* at website http://www.sacred-texts.com.

𝒞hapter 2 , 𝒯he 𝒞laiming of 𝒜tlantis   99

1. Kenneth L. Feder, *Frauds, Myths and Mysteries: Science and Pseudoscience in Archaeology,* 3rd ed., CA: Mayfield Publishing, 1999, pp. 159-182.

2. Helena P. Blavatsky (1831-1891), Theosophy Magazine, Vol. 66, No. 8, June, 1978 (Pages 235-238; Size: 12K) (Number 2 of a 6-part series) *The Races of Man II: Rounds and Races*.

3. Dr. Doreal, *Interpretation of the Book of Revelation* 6:9-11 – 6:12-17, pp. 15-17. Handout.

4. Plato (427-347 BC), *Critias*. Translated by Benjamin Jowett. NY: Scribner & Sons, 1871. Persons of the Dialogue: Critias, Hermocrates, Timaeus, and Socrates. (360 BCE). ***This is the only written story in ancient***

history mentioning Atlantis. All other literary accounts about Atlantis in history are written based on this fragment. Plato was the son of wealthy and influential Athenian parents. He was a respected student of Socrates and states many times within the dialogues that this story of Atlantis, handed down from his grandfather Critias, is true. Was Plato's story of Atlantis is a fantastical illusion as some scholars say? It was found to be fundamentally impossible to prove that Plato's Atlantis was fiction, although archaeological data does not defend the premise that such sophisticated civilizations existed around 9,000 BC. Until the controversial translation by Dr. Doreal of *The Emerald Tablets of Thoth, The Atlantean,* in 1925, states that Thoth (later Hermes-Thoth) declares to have lived in Atlantis from 50,000 BC, until the third destruction when he (and the remaining Atlanteans) came to Egypt with his incredible knowledge, built the Great Pyramids and the Sphinx (where it is said to house a great spaceship that will one day save Israel from great enemies), until his death around 36,000 BC. Thoth lived 16,000 years. Read more about Thoth in Chapter 5, *Tales of Ancient Egypt, Thoth-Hermes & Mercury.*

5. Ignatius Donnelly, *Atlantis: The Antediluvian World. Part I. The History Of Atlantis,* 1882, pp. 244-45.
6. Angelos Georgiou Galanopoulos & Edward Bacon, *Atlantis: The truth behind the legend.* Indiana: Bobbs-Merrill Co., 1969. This was a Frisian chronicle from the Middle Ages, referring to the disappearance of an ancient land in the ocean. *See also* Charles Berlitz, *Atlantis: The Eighth Continent.* NY: P. Putnam & Sons.

384

7. J. V. Luce, *Lost Atlantis: new light on an old legend.* NY: McGraw-Hill Book Co., 1969. pp. 10-45.
8. Helena P. Blavatsky, Theosophy Magazine, Vol. 66, No. 10, August, 1978, (Pages 300-305; Size: 17K), (Number 4 of a 6-part series), *The Races of Man, IV: The Atlanteans.* The "Belial" mentioned is as noted in Deut. 13:13.
9. Edgar C. Cayce, *Readings: Continent and Culture of Atlantis.* Copyright Edgar Cayce Foundation 1971, 1993-1995.
10. Helena P. Blavatsky, Theosophy Magazine, Vol. 66, No. 10, August, 1978, (Pages 300-305; Size: 17K), (Number 4 of a 6-part series), *The Races of Man, IV: The Atlanteans.*
11. Rainer W. Kühne, *The Location and Dating of Atlantis. See* website at http://www.beepworld.de.

Chapter 3 - Tales of Creation, Emanation & Evolution 181

1. Ramon Gil Barros, *The Story of Noanase.* Parabola: The Magazine of Myth and Tradition, Vol. 23, No. 1, February, 1988, p. 51.
2. Helena P. Blavatsky, Theosophy Magazine, Vol. 24, No.1, November, 1935, p. 27.
3. Swami Krishnananda, *Mandukya Upanishad* 1, 6. The Divine Life Society, Sivananda Ashram, Rishikesh, India.
4. *Koran* 27:15.

5. René Guénon, *The Language of the Birds. Communication of the mystery.* Reprinted in <u>Parabola</u>: The Magazine of Myth and Tradition, Vol. 20, No. 3, August 1995, p. 70.

6. Gil Ramon Barros, *Message to the Younger Brother. Wisdom teachings of the Kaggaba-Wiwa people.* Reprinted in <u>Parabola</u>: The Magazine of Myth and Tradition, Vol. 23, No. 1, February, 1988, p. 51. As told by to Gladys Jimeno, translated from Spanish by Juan Julian Caicedo.

7. Saint Bernard of Clairvaux (1090-1153). *See* website http://encyclopedia.freedictionary.com.

8. *Mark 11:24, KJV, The Holy Bible.*

9. King Solomon, *Ecclesiastes 11*, KJV, *The Holy Bible.*

10. Akkadian version (2350-2200 BCE), *The Story of Atrahasis* (c. 1640 BC).

11. Assyrian version, *Epic Of Gilgamesh.* 7th century BC account of the Great Flood and the story of creation written 1,500 years before the Hebrew's story of creation as told in *Genesis.* These dates have yet to be reconciled.

12. *Matthew 26:53, KJV, The Holy Bible.*

13. Hebrew version, *The Story of the Great Flood,* Genesis 6-8, KJV, *The Holy Bible.*

14. Sumerian version (3100-2000 BCE), *The Epic of Gilgamesh.*

15. Robert Crosbie (1849-1919), reprinted in <u>Theosophy Magazine</u>, Vol. 66, No. 8, June, 1978. Founder of the <u>Theosophy Magazine</u> in 1912. *See* website at *United Lodge of Theosophist, Washington, D.C.,* at http:www/ultdc.org/rc.htm.

16. Helena P. Blavatsky, <u>Theosophy Magazine</u>, Vol. 66, No. 8, June, 1978, (Pages 235-238; Size: 12k) (Number 2 of a 6-Part Series) *The Races Of Man(1) II: Rounds And Races.*

17. Ernst Friedrich Schumacher, <u>Enlightenment Magazine</u>. E. F. Schumacher was born in Germany in 1911. A Rhodes scholar at Oxford in the 1930's, he fled back to England before the Second World War to avoid living under Nazism. *See* website at http://www.wie.org.

18. Chart of the Antediluvian Patriarchs and the Date of the Flood from Genesis. *See* http://www.hammer hosting.com.

19. *Bereshith (Genesis) 1:1, The Torah.*

20. *Sephiroth,* E. E. Rehmus, *The Magician's Dictionary*: *An Apocalyptic Cyclopaedia of Advanced Ma/magi (Kal Arts and Alternate Meanings),* Feral House, 1990. *See* website at http://www.chronozon.com.

21. *Enochian,* E. E. Rehmus, *The Magician's Dictionary*: *An Apocalyptic Cyclopaedia of Advanced Ma/magi (Kal Arts and Alternate Meanings),* Feral House, 1990. (out of print).

22. *Elohim,* Eliphas Levi, *The Nuctameron of the Hebrews. See* website at http://www.mystae.com.

23. Robert Temple, *The Sirius Mystery*, Destiny Books, Rochester, 1997, pp.273-315. Offers an extensive research on the records of fish-tailed water creatures in past civilizations, with particular emphasis on the modern Dogon tribe of Mali, Africa.

24. *Angels,* E. E. Rehmus, *The Magician's Dictionary*: *An Apocalyptic Cyclopaedia of Advanced Ma/magi (Kal Arts and Alternate Meanings),* Feral House, 1990.

25. Arthur Charles Clark, *In Science* for June 5, 1998. Arthur C. Clarke of "2001" fame says in his essay "Presidents, Experts, and Asteroids," pp. 1532-3. You can find more on this subject at the website http://www.holysmoke.org/sdhok/clark.htm.
26. Mark Twain, *Mark Twain's Notebook*, 1896. *See Twainquotes.com,* at http://www.twainquotes.com.

Chapter 4 - The Claiming of Humanity   247

1. Albert Einstein (1875-1955). Physicist and Nobel Prize winner in Physics in 1921 "for his services to Theoretical Physics, and especially for his discovery of the law of the photoelectric effect."
2. Henry Wadsworth Longfellow, Poetry of (1807-1882), *The Seaside and the Fireside: The Builders.*
3. Antoine Court de Gebelin (1728-1784). *See* Paul Christian's *The History and Practice of Magic.* NJ: Citadel Press, 1972, pp. 143-144. Gebelin was a French scholar and son of Antoine Court.
4. Sir Isaac Newton. *See* Henry Thomas and Dana Lee Thomas' *Living Biographies of Great Scientists.* Illustrations by Gordon Ross. Garden City, NY: Blue Ribbons Books, 1946, pp. 51-65.
5. Vincent Van Gogh (1853-1890). Dutch Post-Impressionist Painter.
6. Paul Valery (1871-1945), *Collected Works.*
7. Charles Burchfield (1893-1967). American scene painter and poet.

8. Jerome Rothenberg, *Technicians of the Sacred: A Range of Poetries from Africa, America, Asia, Europe and Oceania, Second edition, Revised and Expanded.* This is part of an ancient Aztec song.

9. Honoré de Balzac, *The Magic Skin*. NY: Charles Scribner's Sons, 1914, p. 75.

10. James Russell Lowell (1819-1891), *The Present Crisis.* One of the group of authors sometimes called the Fireside Poets, or the Schoolroom Poets, a group of which Henry Wadsworth Longfellow, John Greenleaf Whittier, and Oliver Wendell Holmes were an integral part.

11. Henry Ward Beecher (1813-1887), *Progress of Thought in the Church,* The North American Review, Vol. 135, Issue 309 (August 1882). Preacher, orator, lecturer, writer, editor, and reformer, was born at Litchfield, Connecticut, in 1813.

12. Ralph Waldo Emerson (1803-1882), *Essays*. NY: Grosset & Dunlap, no date (First Series, 1841), p. 30.

13. William Ellery Channing (1780-1842), *Address on Self-Culture*. Excerpt from Esther J. Tribble's *A Handbook of Literature*, 1882.

14. Stephen Vincent Benet, *The Making of a Dream.* Quoted from the editor of TIME Magazine, Alexander Eliot's *Three Hundred Years of American Painting,* 1957, p. 1.

15. Plato (427-347 BC). *See Memorable Quotations* at website http://www.memorablequotations.com.

16. Khalil Gibran (1883-1931). Lebanese-American philosophical essayist, novelist, mystical poet, and artist. *See* http://encyclopedia.freedictionary.com.

17. Roger Bacon (1212-1292). Quotation taken from Henry Thomas and Dana Lee Thomas' *Living Biographies of Great Scientists*, NY: Blue Ribbon Books, 1946, pp. 13-20.
18. Lord Francis Bacon (1572-1625), *Essay on Studies.*
19. Madame Marie Curie (1867-1934) (born Marie 'nicknamed Manya' Sklodovska-Curie) in Warsaw, Poland. She was one of the greatest scientists of the century. She had degrees in mathematics and physics. Winner of two Nobel Prizes, for Physics in 1903 and for Chemistry in 1911, she performed pioneering studies with radium and polonium and contributed profoundly to the understanding of radioactivity. *See* website at http://hum.amu.edu.pl. *See also* Henry Thomas and Dana Lee Thomas' *Living Biographies of Great Scientists*, NY: Blue Ribbon Books, 1946, pp. 263-280.
20. Ludwig Von Beethoven (1770-1827).
21. Sir Thomas More (1478-1535), *Utopia*, of their laws.
22. Roger Ascham (1515-1568), *The Schoolmaster,* 1570.
23. Lord Francis Bacon (1573-1625), *Essay on Truth.*
24. John Lyly (1554-1606), *Euphues: the Anatomy of Wit,* 1578.
25. John Milton (1608-1674), *Areopagitica.*
26. Jaina Sutras (trans.) from the *PrakRti* by Hermann Jacobi, 1884, from the *Sacred Books of the East.*
27. Eminent scholar of Gnosticism, Elaine Pagels. Excerpt from *An Introduction To Gnosticism and The Nag Hammadi Library.*
28. Ellen Boye, *Grönland.* Samarbejde rundt om Nordpolen, Copenhagen, 1974, pp. 65-70. *See* John H.

Bodley. *Victims of Progress*, 4th ed. CA: Mayfield Publishing, 1972, p. 165.

29. Leonard Crow Dog (1942), *American Myths and Legends*. A Native American (Sioux) author. Leonard Crow Dog was the spiritual leader of the American Indian Movement of the 1960's and 1970's and served time in prison as a result of his political activities. He was born in 1942 on the Rosebud Reservation. Recorded by Richard Erodes, from *American Myths and Legends*. Reprinted in <u>Parabola</u>: The Magazine of Myth and Tradition.

30. John H. Wellington, Newspaper Article, <u>German Southwest Africa</u>, 1901, *Southwest Africa and Its Human Issues*, Oxford: Clarendon Press/Oxford University Press, 1967. *See* John H. Bodley, *Victims of Progress*, 4th ed, CA: Mayfield Publishing, 1972.

31. Rene Maunier, *The Sociology of the Colonies,* Vol. 2. London: Routledge and Paul Kegan, 1949, p. 513. *See* John H. Bodley, *Victims of Progress*, 4th ed, CA: Mayfield Publishing, 1972, p. 99.

32. Max Ehrmann (1872-1945), *Desiderata*, MA: Bruce Humphries Publishing Company of Boston, 1948.

33. David Appelbaum, *Can War Be Stopped?* <u>Parabola:</u> The Magazine of Myth and Tradition, (27) (4), Winter (2002), p. 32. *See* also *Yoga Sutra*.

34. Fariduddin 'Attar (1130-1230). See http://zensufi.com.

35. S. Palacios i. Mendiburu, *Boletin de la Sociedad Geografica de Lima*, 1892, pp. 289-290. *See* John H. Bodley, *Victims of Progress*, 4th ed, CA: Mayfield Publishing, 1972, p. 36.

36. Miguel Nostradamus. *See* John Hogue, *Nostradamus & The Millinenum: Predictions of the Future,* Garden City, NJ: Doubleday, 1987.

37. German Professor Boon, in lecture to the Royal Colonial Institute of London, 1914. *Citing* John H. Wellington, *Southwest Africa and Its Human Issues*, Oxford: Clarendon Press/Oxford University Press, 1967, p. 204. *See* John H. Bodley, *Victims of Progress*, 4th ed, CA: Mayfield Publishing, 1972, p. 54.

38. Plato (427-347 BC), *Phaedo* (360 BC), (trans) Benjamin Jowett.

39. Ron Crocombe, *New Guinea*, 1968, 3(3) pp. 39-49. Bougainville, Copper, R.R.A. and secessionism. *See* John H. Bodley, *Victims of Progress*, 4th ed, CA: Mayfield Publishing, 1972, p. 143.

40. *Bhagavad-Gita*, xviii. 59.

41. Persian saying.

42. Miguel Chase-Sardi & Adolpho Colombres, *Por la Liberación del Indigena, Buenos Aires: Ediciones del Sol.* 1975, p. 240. *See* John H. Bodley, *Victims of Progress*, 4th ed. CA: Mayfield Publishing, 1972, p. 166.

43. *Easter Island,* E. E. Rehmus, *The Magician's Dictionary: An Apocalyptic Cyclopaedia of Advanced Ma/magi (Kal Arts and Alternate Meanings)*, Feral House, 1990.

44. *The Dene Declaration*, Mel Watkins, *Dene Nation-the Colony Within,* Toronto: University of Toronto Press, 1977. *See* John H. Bodley, *Victims of Progress*, 4th ed. CA: Mayfield Publishing, 1972,   p. 145.

45. *Unidad Indigena* (1975) 1(1):1. Since 1971, at least five regional Indian organizations have emerged in Columbia. As with the Shuar in Ecuador, the primary focus of all of these organizations has been to fight for control of traditional Indian lands, for traditional forms of organization, and for their language and culture. These activities and organizations are covered by a national distributed newspaper, *Unidad Indigena. See* John H. Bodley, *Victims of Progress*, 4th ed. CA: Mayfield Publishing, 1972, p. 154.
46. Aristotle (384-322 BC), Greek philosopher. *See* madwed.com/quotations.
47. Akhenaten (1370-1336 BC), Egyptian Pharaoh and founder of a brief monotheistic religion. *See Freeman Institute* at website http://www.freemaninstitute.com.
48. Thomas Paine. Quote taken from Alexander Eliot's *Three Hundred Years of American Painting,* 1957.

Chapter 5 - Tales of Ancient Egypt, Thoth, Hermes & Mercury 301

1. Aubrey De Sélincourt (trans.), *Arrian: The Campaigns of Alexander*. Revised with new introduction and notes by J. R. Hamilton, Penguine Books, New York, 1971, p. 264.
2. William Kingsland, *The Great Pyramid in Fact and in Theory*. Peter Tompkins, *The Secrets of the Great Pyramid,* Harper & Row Publishers, New York, 1971, p 284. "Spelled out in Hermes' *Asclepius*, Ficino, Paracelsus, Agrippa, Dee, Bacon, Saint Germain and

the Rosicrucian manual *Enchiridon* which outline the actual steps by which adepts could be put in touch with 'angels and the spirits of the dead.'"—Count Alessandro Cagliostro (1743-1795).

3. Manly P. Hall, *Freemasonry and the Ancient Egyptians.* Quotation taken from Peter Tompkins, *The Secrets of the Great Pyramid,* NY: Harper & Row Publishers, 1971, p. 284.

4. William Henry, *The Language of the Birds,* p. 31. *See also* http://www.williamhenry.net.

5. Archimedes (287-212 BC). Henry Thomas and Dana Lee Thomas' *Living Biographies of Great Scientists,* NJ: Blue Ribbon, 1946, pp. 1-10. Archimedes founded the Law of Specific Gravity known today as the *Principle of Archimedes,* briefly stated as follows: "A body immersed in a fluid loses as much in weight as the weight of an equal volume of fluid."

6. *Grades of the Ancient and Primitive Memphis-Misraim Rite of Freemasonry. See* the website at http://www.freemasonry.com.

7. Iamblichus (250-325), *Treatise, On the [Egyptian] Mysteries. See Esoterica Archives* at http://www.esotericarchives.com.

8. Sir E. A. Wallis Budge (1857-1934), *The Egyptian Book of the Dead, The Papyrus of Ani.* Sir E. A. Wallis Budge (1857-1934), (trans) *The Book of the Dead.* University Books, New York, 1960, p. 379. *The Table of Destiny,* of the things which have been made, and of the things which shall be made featured also in the Egyptian *Papyrus of Ani.* (240 BC). E. A. Wallis Budge was the Curator of Egyptian and Assyrian Antiquities at

the British Museum from 1894 to 1924. *See* http://www.crystalinks.com.

9. Count Alessandro Cagliostro (1743-1795). *See* Paul Christian, *The History and Practice of Magic*, NJ: Citadell Press, 1972, pp. 81-172.

10. Osiris Onnophris (c. 2400 BC), son of Ra, King of Egypt. *See Free Dictionary*, at website http://www. freedictionary.com.

11. *Dream Stele of Tuthmosis.* "Between the enormous paws is a stele that records a dream Tuthmosis IV had when he was a prince. He dreamt that he stopped to rest in the shadow of the Sphinx during a hunting expedition in the desert. While asleep, the Sphinx spoke to him, saying that he would become king if he cleared away the sand that all but buried the Sphinx. When he became king, Tuthmosis IV cleared the sand and erected a stele that tells the story of his dream. After the work was completed, a chapel was built next to the Sphinx to venerate this sun god." *See Free Dictionary*, at http://www.freedictionary.com.

12. Plato (427-347 BC), *Republic, Book IX. See Sacred Text* website at http://www.sacred-text.com.

13. Aleister Crowley, *Liber Aleph,* Chapter 157, *On the Dragon, which is the Eagle, Serpent and Scorpion.*

14. Aleister Crowley, *Liber Aleph part 7. See Occultopedia, An Encyclopedia of Occultism and the Unexplained,* by Marcus Gay at website http://www. occultopedia.com.

15. Sigmund Freud, *Moses and Monotheism,* 1938. Sigismund Schlomo Freud was born of Jewish descent in Freiburg, Moravia, Austria-Hungary (now the Czech Republic). An Austrian psychiatrist and founder of

psychoanalysis, he was the most influential psychological theorist of 20th-century. Freud once stated: "The only unnatural sexual behavior is none at all." It is often asserted that Freud "discovered" the unconscious mind. "The interpretation of dreams is the royal road to a knowledge of the unconscious activities of the mind." —S. Freud, *The Interpretation of Dreams*, 1900.

16. Mike Fillon, *Science Solves the Ancient Mysteries of the Bible*, Popular Mechanics, Dec. 1996.

17. *Osiris, Occultopedia, The Encyclopedia of Occultism and the Unexplained* at website http://www.occult opedia.com.

18. E. E. Rehmus, *Baghdad, The Magician's Dictionary*: An Apocalyptic Cyclopaedia of Advanced Ma/magi (Kal Arts and Alternate Meanings), (out of print). *See* website at http://www.chronozon.com.

19. Manly P. Hall, *Freemasonry and the Ancient Egyptians.* Quotation taken from Peter Tompkins, *The Secrets of the Great Pyramid,* NY: Harper & Row Publishers, 1971, p. 284.

20. William Kingsland, *The Great Pyramid in Fact and in Theory. See* Peter Tompkins, *The Secrets of the Great Pyramid,* NY: Harper & Row Publishers, 1971, p. 284.

21. Tod Harris, *The Word Made Flesh,* Parabola: The Magazine of Myth & Tradition, Vol. 20, No. 3, August 1995, p.16.

22. Sir E. A. Wallis Budge (1857-1934), *The Egyptian Book of the Dead, The Papyrus of Ani. See* the website http://www.crystalinks.com.

23. Anthony S. Mercatante, *Who's Who in Egyptian*

Mythology, NY: Potter, 1978, pp. 32-33, second edition edited and Copyright in 1995 by Robert Steven Bianchi.

24. Dr. Doreal, (trans.) *The Emerald Tables of Thoth, The Atlantean, Tablet I*, 1925. Dr. Doreal, who has a connection with the Great White Lodge, which also works through the Pyramid Priest-hood, was instructed to recover and return to the Great Pyramid, these Ancient Tablets. Some thirteen hundred years BC, Egypt, the ancient Khem, was in turmoil and many delegations of priests were sent to other parts of the world. Among these were some of the pyramid priests who carried with them the Emerald Tablets as a talisman by which they could exercise authority over the less advanced priest-craft of races descended from other Atlantean colonies. The tablets were understood from legend to give the bearer authority from Thoth. The particular group of priests bearing the tablets emigrated to South America where they found a flourishing race, the Mayas who remembered much of the ancient wisdom. Among these, the priests settled and remained. In the tenth century, the Mayas had thoroughly settled the Yucatan, and the tablets were placed beneath the altar of one of the great temples of the Sun God. After the conquest of the Mayas by the Spaniards, the cities were abandoned and the treasures of the temples forgotten. It should be understood that the Great Pyramid of Egypt has been and still is a temple of initiation into the mysteries. Jesus, Solomon, Apollonius and others were initiated there. This was accomplished, but before returning them, Doreal was given permission to translate and retain a copy of the

wisdom engraved on the Tablets. This was done in 1925, and now, permission has been given for this translation by Doreal to be published solely through the, Brotherhood of the White Temple. This is the only authorized, original and true rendition of these *Emerald Tablets*. It is expected that many will scoff, yet the true student will read between the lines and gain wisdom. If the light is in you, the light which is engraved in the Tablets will respond. —Brotherhood of the White Temple. *See* http://www.bw temple.org.

25. Thoth, Dr. Doreal (trans.) of *The Emerald Tablet No. 1, The History of Atlantis. See* http://www.emerald tablets and http://www.crystalinks. com.

26. Hermes-Thoth, *Hundred Aphorisms*. Also recalled by Ptolemy in *Tetrabiblion.* Quotation taken from Paul Christian, *The History and Practice of Magic,* NJ: Citadell Press, 1972, pp. 81-90.

27. Sir James George Frazer, *The Golden Bough: A study in Magic and Religion,* Vol. I., Abridged Edition, NY: MacMillan, 1951.

28. Thoth. Dr. Doreal (trans.), *Emerald Tablet No. 5, The Dwellers of Unal. See* http://www.emeraldtablets.com.

29. King Ashurbanipal of Assyria (668-627 BC). See Ancient History website at http://www.ancient history.about.com.

30. Hermes-Thoth, Paul Christian's *The History and Practice of Magic*, NJ: Citadell Press, 1972, p. 81.

31. Hermes Trismegistus, *Corpus Hermeticum. See* website at http://www.mystica.com.

32. Anthony S. Mercatante, *Who's Who in Egyptian Mythology,* NY: Potter, 1978. Second edition edited and Copyright in 1995 by Robert Steven Bianchi.

33. The Speech of Thoth, *The Pymander.* Quotation taken from Paul Christian, *The History and Practice of Magic,* NJ: Citadell Press, 1972, pp. 81-90.

34. Thoth, *Emerald Tablet No. 13, Keys to Life and Death.* *See* website at http://www.emeraldtablets.com.

35. Thoth, *Emerald Tablet No. 14, Supplemental*

36. *SHAZAM,* Copyright Marvel Enterprises, Inc., NY: 1940-41.

37. *The Goddess Isis. Occultopedia, An Encyclopedia of Occultism and the Unexplained,* by Marcus Gay at the website http://www.occultopedia.com.

38. Apollonius of Tyana. *Doctrine of Apollonius of Tyana.* Excerpt from Paul Christian (1811-1877), *The History and Practice of Magic*, NJ: Citadel, 1972. French occultist, best known for his *Histoire de la Magie*, 1870, pp. 211-212.

Additional References and Reading   399

Bertrand Russell, *History of Philosophy*

G. H. Lewes, *Biographical History of Philosophy*

Shaikh Sharfuddin Maneri, *Letters from a Sufi Teacher*

H. P. Blavatsky, *The Secret Doctrine, Isis Unveiled*

C. G. Jung, *The Secret of the Golden Flower, The Sanskrit Vedas, The Zend Avesta,* and *The Shastabad*

H. S. Bellamy, *Built Before the Flood*

I. Velikovsky, *Worlds in Collision*

Athanasius Kircher, *Voyage Ecstatique, Mundus
    Subterraneus*

Honore de Balzac, *Etudes Philosophiques (Serafita)*

Court de Gebelin, *Plan General du Monde Primitif*

Claudius Ptolemy *'de Peluse', The Great Construction*

Eliphas Levi: *History of Magic, Histoire de la Kabbale*

Francis Ban-att, *Abramelin the Magus*

M. A. Attwood, *A Suggestive Inquiry into the Hermetic
    Mystery, Clacivula Salmonis, [also in English: The
    Keys of Solomon the King]*

Jacques Gafferel, *Mysteries of the Divine Qabala and
    Forgotten Curiosities of the Persian Talismanic Art*

Also works by Agrippa, Philalethes, Democretus, Dupotet

A. E. Wake, *Hermetic and Alchemical Writings of
    Paracelsus, Theophrastus Paracelsus*

'Lucia', *Life of Cagliostro and Count Cagliostro*

Court de Gebelin, *Memoirs [unpublished]*

E. Loth, *Emblems of the 33 Degrees*

Herodotus, Diodorus Siculus, Plutarch, Migne,

Paul Christian, *Heroes of Christianity Throughout the Ages*

Sir E. Wallis Budge, *The Dwellers on the Nile*

Arthur Weigall, *Akhnaten*

St. Jerome, *Prefaces*

The teachings of Thoth-Hermes *recorded in the Pymander
    and in Concerning Thrice-Greatest Hermes; The
    Asclepios, Patricius, Nova de Universis Philosophia
    and The Hundred Aphorisms of Thoth-Hermes, Thrice
    Greatest Hermes*